Intermediate
To Serger

© Copyright 2019 - All rights reserved.

It is not legal to reproduce, duplicate, or transmit any part of this document in either electronic means or in printed format. Recording of this publication is strictly prohibited and any storage of this document is not allowed unless with written permission from the publisher except for the use of brief quotations in a book review.

Table of Contents

Introduction iv

Chapter One: Blind Hem Serging Technique 6

Chapter Two: How To Use A Gathering Foot 18

Chapter Three: Maintenance of Serger Machine 28

Chapter Four: How To Make Baby Blanket 35

Chapter Five: How To Make Your Own Pillow Covers 42

Chapter Six: How to Make Drawstring Bag Using Serger Machine 47

Chapter Seven: Dust Cover For A Serger Machine ... 69

Chapter Eight: Christmas Stocking 84

Chapter Nine: Snack Bags 98

Chapter Ten: Holiday Tree Napkin 117

Chapter Eleven: How To Make Face Mask 142

Final Words 178

Introduction

In this intermediate guide to serging, you will learn advanced techniques that you can use to make several knit garments. Most of the DIY projects are much easier to do with a serger machine.

One of the greatest benefits of the serger machine is to learn how to make blind hems. In most of your garments, you want to create an invisible stitch from the outside. In this tutorial, you will learn how to use the blind hem technique to create a deep hem for your pants, skirts, and unlined jackets.

You will also learn how to install the blind hem foot, adjust the tension, and needle threads for you to create a perfect stitch for joining two folded edges of the fabric.

Another important foot for any serger is the gathering foot. If you love to create a lot of gathers in your garment Projects, you will be able to learn how to use the gathering foot and an example Project you can work out with to make gathers. Depending on the task you want to do, you can invest in an appropriate foot and make garments that have a professional look.

You will also learn how to take care of your overlock machine and extend its lifetime. Regular maintenance of the machine is very important to keep your machine clean and improve its performance. An accumulation of dust and fill up of threads and trims inside the machine can lower the performance of your machine. This manual will teach you to regularly clean and oil the different parts of the machine.

You will also know how to make simple DIY projects using different stitches and features in your machine. Some of the simple DIY projects you will learn to make at the end of this tutorial include: sewing a personalized baby blanket, sewing a pillow cover, serging a drawstring bag, sewing a dust cover for your overlock machine, sewing a Christmas stocking, sewing a holiday napkin tree, and sewing your own face mask.

These are personalized serging projects you can do with your machine. You will learn the step-by-step procedures on how to sew each of the projects. Some of them are very easy and they will not take you a lot of time to sew them. These projects are also budget-friendly since you can make some of them from scrap fabrics.

You will also be able to add your personal touch to the projects. Once you learn how to sew these different DIY garment projects, you can give them a gift to your friends and loved ones.

Get ready to learn on your next serging project!

Chapter One:
Blind Hem Serging Technique

Did you know you can make super clean hems with your serger machine? Although you can make blind hem with your sewing machine, the serger sewing technique is a super-fast and easy way to hem your fabrics and give your hems a clean finish. For this reason, a serger machine dominates the regular sewing machine making it the most preferred for excellent sewing projects.

A blind hem is a technique used to create a blind stitch on a cloth with little visible threads on the front side of the cloth. A blind stitch helps create an invisible stitch thread by joining two pieces of fabric together. These invisible stitches are hidden under the folded edges of the fabric.

When you use blind hem stitches, the thread is invisible at the front of your garment and almost hidden on the inside of the garment. This sewing technique ensures the stitches remain hidden inside the fabric hem.

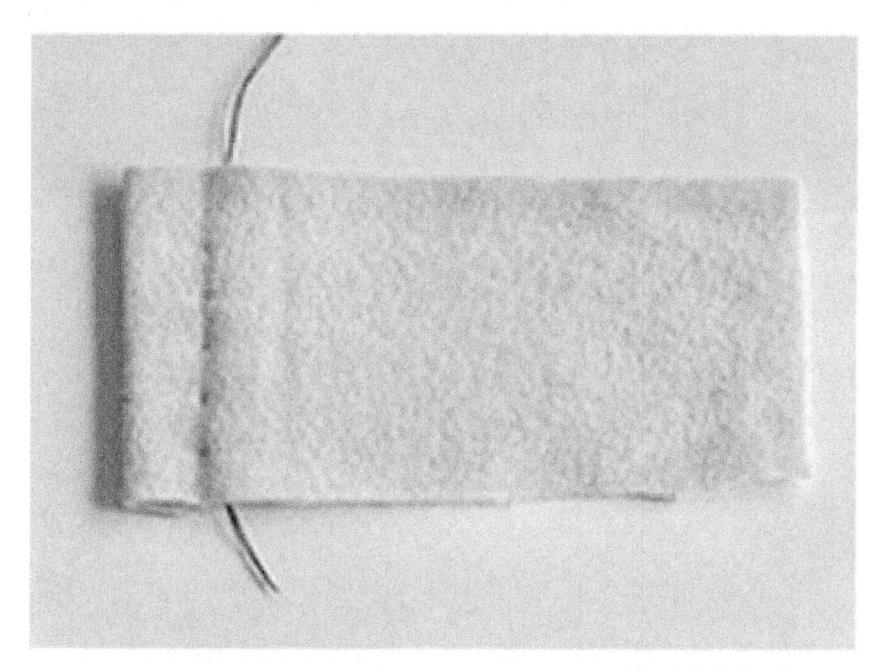

Outside with invisible seam

When using a serger machine to create invisible hems, ensure the fabric stretch remains natural.

You can use this technique to attach pockets and trimmings to your garment.

If you're using a regular sewing machine to create a blind hem, you need a presser foot and then select the stitch pattern suitable for sewing blind hems. A zigzag stitch can be used to create a blind stitch using the sewing machine.

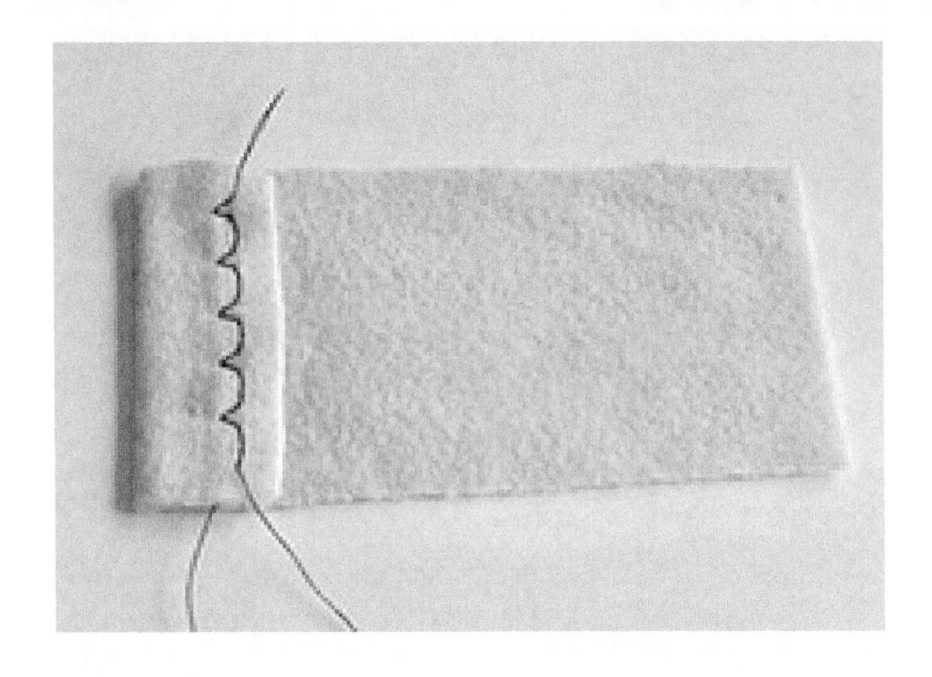

Inside with zigzag stitch

How to use a Serger machine to create a blind hem

In just one move, you can serge the edges of the fabric, trim, and stitch it at the same time! Your serger machine allows you to do that all in one easy step.

Requirements:

1. Thick threads for your looper
2. Ballpoint needles
3. Blind Hem foot presser
4. Fabric you want to do serging on

Blind hem foot

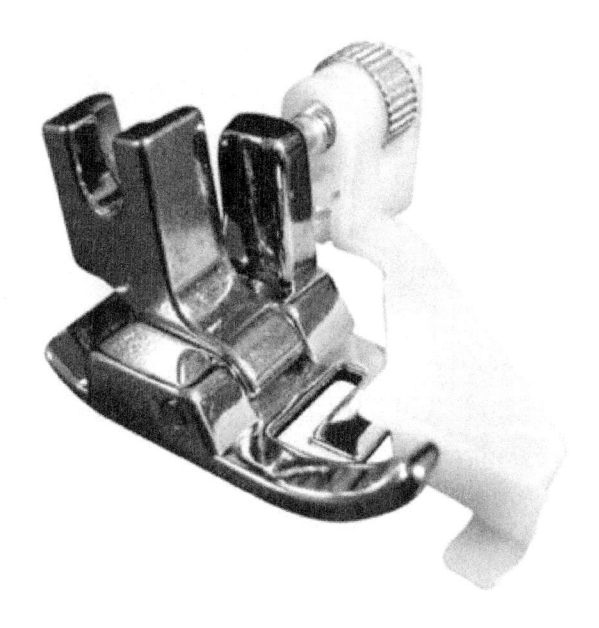

This universal adjustable blind hem foot is designed to fit in most overlock models. It helps you sew neat and professional looking stitches. This foot is suitable for creating blind stitches on your skirts, trousers, and jackets.

When stitching, the bulk stitches are sewn on the hem while the larger jump stitch moves across to attach to the hem of the fabric on the wrong side up.

Before you begin to use the foot, you should match the stitch position with the available hem fabric in three ways:

- Adjust the foot using the metal screw and move the plastic plate to the left and right.

- Adjust the stitch width

- Adjust the needle position (although this applies to selected serger machines)

The foot has a metal guide at the center and three grooves located on the underside. When blind hemming, the fold of your garment snugly fits against the metal guide in the foot. This maintains the accuracy of the stitch on the edges while the underneath grooves prevent slipping of the garment.

The needle will swing over the metal guide in order to create slack in the upper looper tension and as a result, you create an invisible stitch on your garment.

Match the folded fabric with the plastic guide. You can also adjust jump stitch nibbles to feed on a small amount of the fabric. If you set a larger nibble, you will have a larger stitch on the right side of the hem.

Blind hem foot not only creates blind hemstitches at the bottom of your skirts and jackets, you can also use it to make a perfect topstitch on garments. If you're using it to add a topstitch, ensure the guide is up and lined with the outside edges of the fabric.

You can also use this foot when creating seams around the neckline, the arm cycles, or creating a bodice on your skirt using a topstitch.

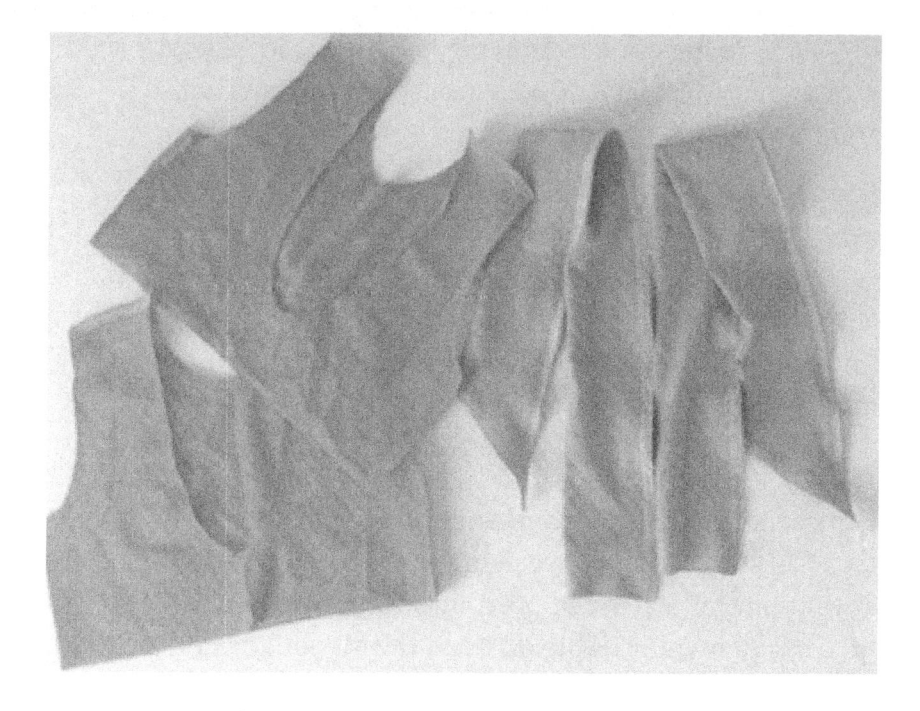

Steps to create a blind hem stitch

Step 1

Insert a ballpoint needle for sewing knits into your fabric. A ballpoint needle is used for sewing special fabrics. Insert the needle in the needle bar clamp and fasten the screws. Ensure the long groove faces the side where you thread the needle.

Step 2

Take your blind Hem Foot presser and attach it to the stock foot presser of your machine. Put the top thread underneath and pull both threads to the back. Adjust the screw on your blind hem foot presser to adjust the stitch width according to your need.

This can be done by moving the gauge either left or right. You can also test it first to ensure you have moved it to a good position.

Step 3

Adjust your needle settings based on the type of fabric you're using or when you want a different stitch length. In this example, we are going to adjust the settings to sew a narrow hem in our fabric.

This is just a standard serging process so we will not adjust the stitch length or do anything to the differential feed. To start with, we are using the left needle so we need to lower your left needle to position 1. You can even set it to zero based on how tight you need the stitches but the best setting is usually 0 to 2. We are not going to use the right needle.

Make sure to thread the needle with a color that matches the fabric you're sewing. This ensures the little stitches that appear at the front (right side) of the fabric are hardly visible.

You can also use different colors for the looper thread because the stitches usually show on the inside.

Strengthen or tighten the upper looper by increasing the tension to 6 and then decrease the tension of the lower looper by 3.

Step 4

Take your fabric and double-fold it. You will sew on the wrong side of the fabric.

Folded piece of fabric

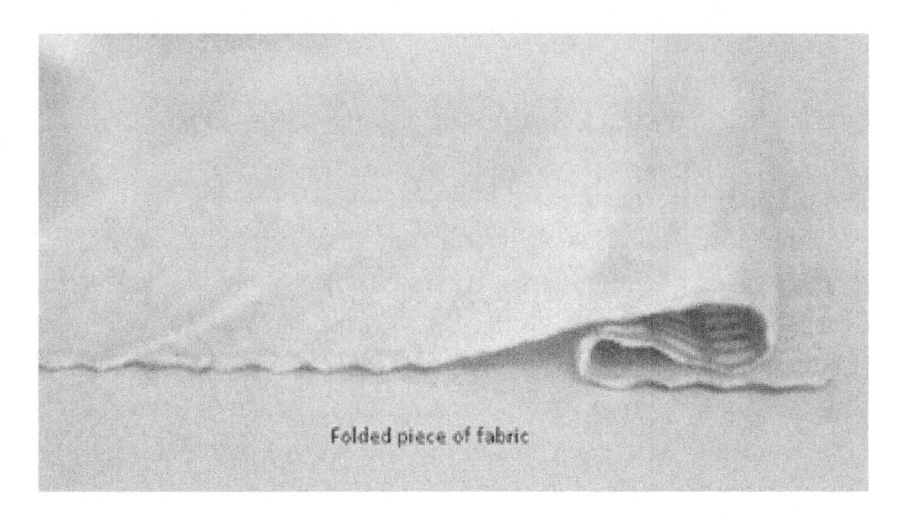

Step 5

Flip the fabric and get ready to feed it to the serger machine.

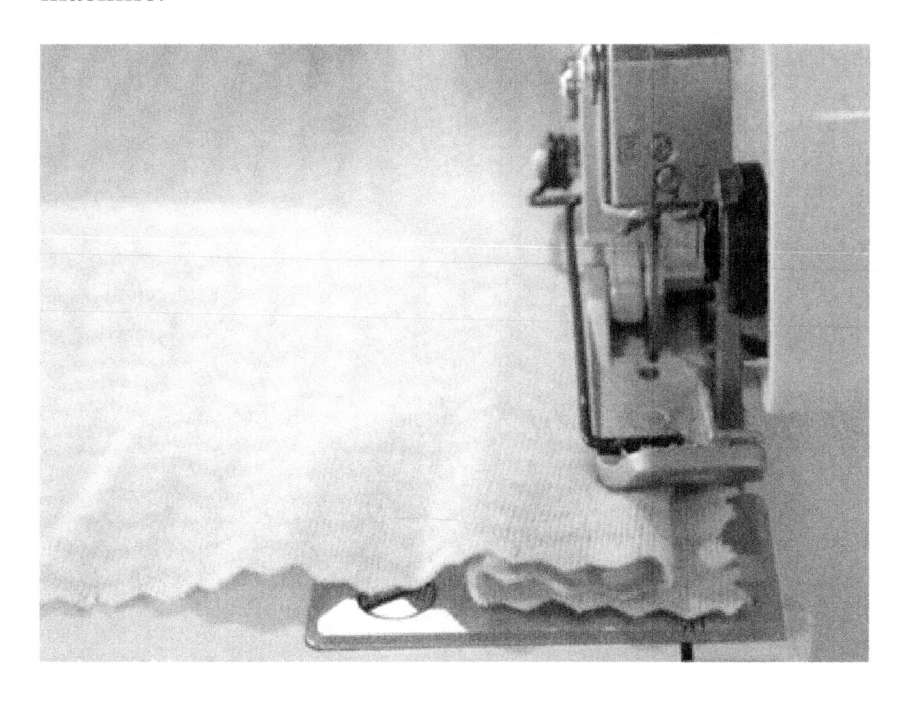

Step 6

Place the wrong side of the fabric facing up. Then, feed the fabric such that the folded edge is on the left.

Position your presser foot on the hem so that the needle stitches right at the edges of the fold while the blade cuts the excess fabric. The blind hem presser foot has a metal guide at the center of the presser foot and three grooves underneath. The metal guide ensures you accurately feed the fabric underneath the presser foot while the groove prevents the fabric from slipping.

The closer the needle pierce to the edge of the fabric, the smaller the stitch on the right side of the fabric.

Step 7

You can set the serger speed to medium and start to stitch! While stitching, don't pull the fabric or stretch it. Leave it to feed through!

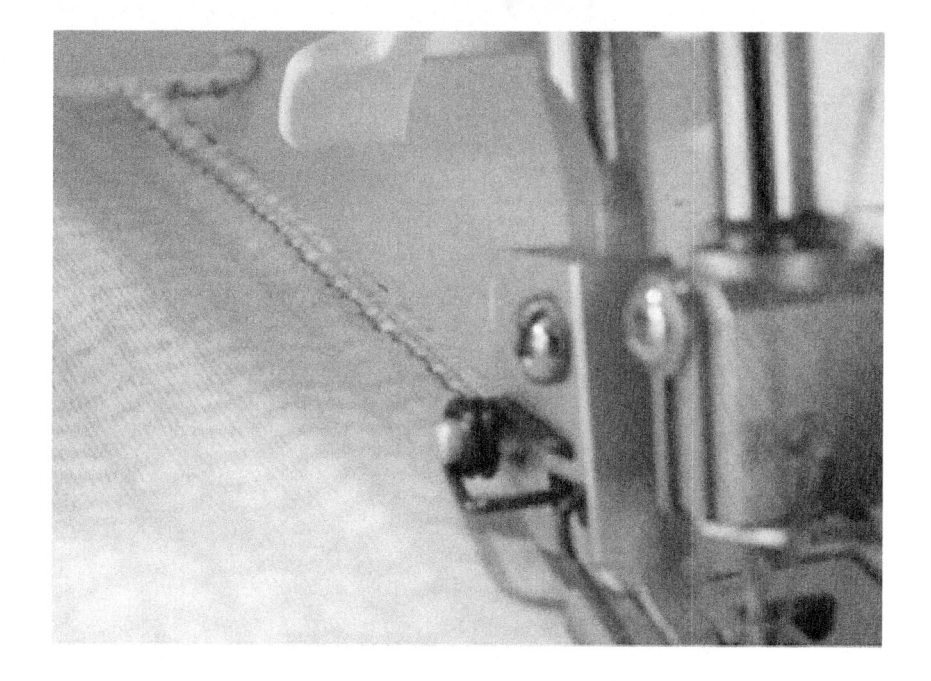

Step 8

After stitching, leave a long chain so that your machine does not come undone.

With these simple steps, you can sew a blind hem to your fabric.

Chapter Summary

The blind hem serging technique is a great way of creating hidden stitches. These stitches can be used when creating pockets or when you want to add decorative stitches on a piece of garment.

Based on the type of serging machine you're using, you can change the settings to have blind hem stitch, choose your stitch length and then go ahead to stitch.

When stitching the garment, avoid pulling it or stretching it because this can result in irregular stitches. Just let it feed through.

Make sure to use a thread that matches your fabric color so that the stitches remain invisible.

In the next chapter, you will learn how to use a gathering tool.

Chapter Two:
How To Use A Gathering Foot

If you have been sewing ruffles and gathers a lot then a gathering foot will be a great accessory to your sewing.

A gathering foot will make your work easier and give you excellent results. No one can say no to sewing on a perfectly gathered skirt! The art of making gathers evenly makes your project look awesome.

In this chapter, I will show you how to use a gathering tool to create gathers on your project. Regular sewing machines can also use gathering tools to create gathers or fabric ruffles. Whether using your sewing machine or serger machine, it works the same.

What is a gathering foot?

A gathering foot is a great sewing tool that allows you to automatically create a gathered ruffle. It looks like the regular presser foot but due to the shape of the foot, it gathers as you sew the fabric.

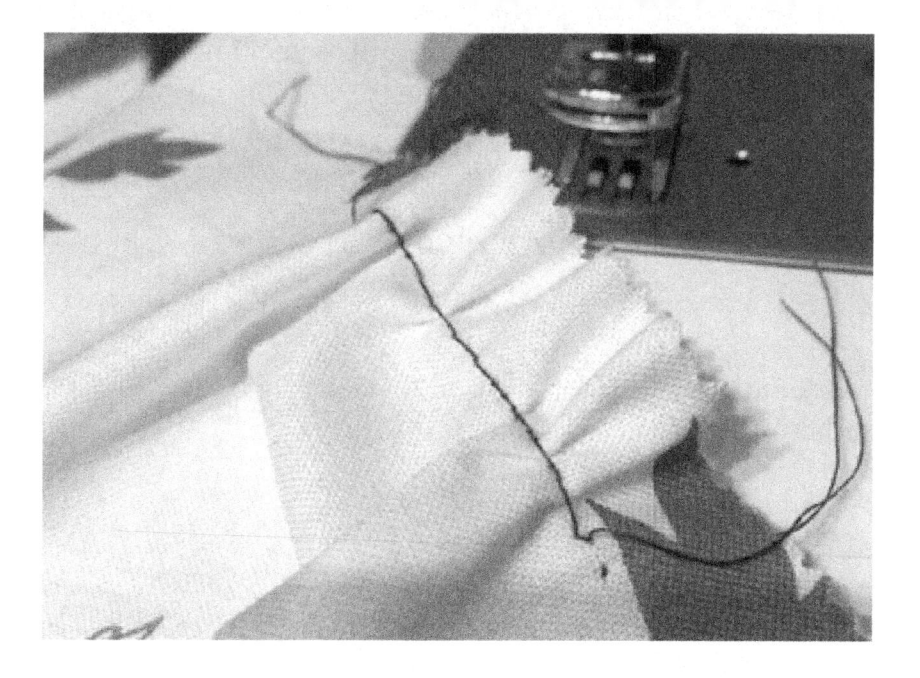

A gathering foot works well with finer fabrics otherwise it will not work well with thick fabrics.

If you love creating gathers on your project, invest in this gathering tool, and get ready to produce fine and soft even gathers.

In addition, you don't have to worry about sliding up and down the stitch line as you sew gathers. You can even sew gathers on the second layer of fabric with just a single pass.

A gathering tool can gather stitches in a piece of fabric alone or it can gather while attaching the gathers to a flat piece of fabric (non-ruffled fabric).

You can use a gathering foot in three ways:

1. To gather/ruffle fabric alone

2. To gather/ruffle fabric and at the same time sew it on a piece of non-ruffled fabric

3. To shirr using elastic thread

How to gather the fabric alone

Step 1

Remove the presser foot and replace it with the gathering foot in your machine

Step 2

Adjust your stitch length. If you want to have more gathers in your garment, you have to increase the stitch length. You can practice with different stitch lengths before you settle on your perfect stitch length for your gathers.

You can also adjust the tension dials for better results. Increasing the tension will enable you to gather more tightly.

Hold the thread tails before you start sewing to prevent them from being caught underneath.

Step 3

Place your piece of fabric underneath the foot and lower the foot down. Go ahead and sew gathers on the fabric. Do not pull the fabric or push it while sewing, let it feed through.

Based on the stitch length you will notice neat and even gathers. You can trim the fabric to have your desired size.

Unlike traditional methods of sewing gathers, a gathering foot allows you to stitch just one line and you don't have to pull the threads once you have finished sewing.

Note: The thickness of the fabric affects the distribution of gathers on the fabric. Heavy fabrics are very difficult to gather with gathering feet but you can easily do them using the ruffler foot. Gathering feet are suitable for fine fabrics.

How to gather fabric and at the same time sew it to a non-gathered fabric

Step 1

Replace the standard presser foot with the gathering foot tool.

Step 2

Set your stitch length very high. You can set it to the maximum level of your machine and tighten the upper tension looper for you to obtain fuller gathers.

Step 3

Place the fabric that needs to be gathered underneath the foot and then lower the gathering foot. Place the fabric that is to be unruffled at the center slot of the gathering foot. The right side of the fabric should face down.

Go ahead and create gathers at the same time sewing unruffled fabric. Hold the unruffled fabric when sewing and pull it slightly to the right to prevent it from slipping out.

This results in evenly distributed gathers attached to a non-gathered fabric. You can trim any excess gathered fabric on the sides giving your garment a great finish.

How to shirr using gathering foot

A gathering foot can also be used as a shirring foot because it can be used to make shirred effects using an elastic thread on your bobbin. The shirring effect improves the texture of your fabric and makes it look more beautiful.

You can create puckered shirred effects by sewing several rows of gathering stitches.

You need to hand wind your bobbin using a loosely thin elastic thread. Don't stretch the thread. Insert the top thread in your sewing needle and bring up the elastic thread. Push the threads to the back and start sewing.

If you want to sew small gathers then make the stitch length short but if you need full gathers, make the stitch length long.

After adding gathering stitches on several rows, you can use a steam iron on the stitched rows. Just place the iron with the steam over your fabric and the shirring will shrink up to create a good shirr effect.

You can practice this on a piece of fabric scrap before you sew these shirring gatherings on your final fabric. This will help you determine how much fabric you need for you to create the desired shirring and gathers. It will also help you know how tight you need to adjust the tension and how long the stitch length is.

Gathering using a Serger machine

Gathering with a serger machine is much faster and easier. Once you know how to gather using your serger, you will never go back to using your normal sewing machine to create gathers.

When gathering using a serger machine, you don't need a special foot tool or any attachments. All you have to do is adjust the stitch length and change the setting to the differential feeding system.

Step 1

Set your serger to have 4 thread serging.

Step 2

Increase differential feed to the highest number. In this case, we will use 2. Increase your stitch length to have the highest number. Some sergers have up to number 5.

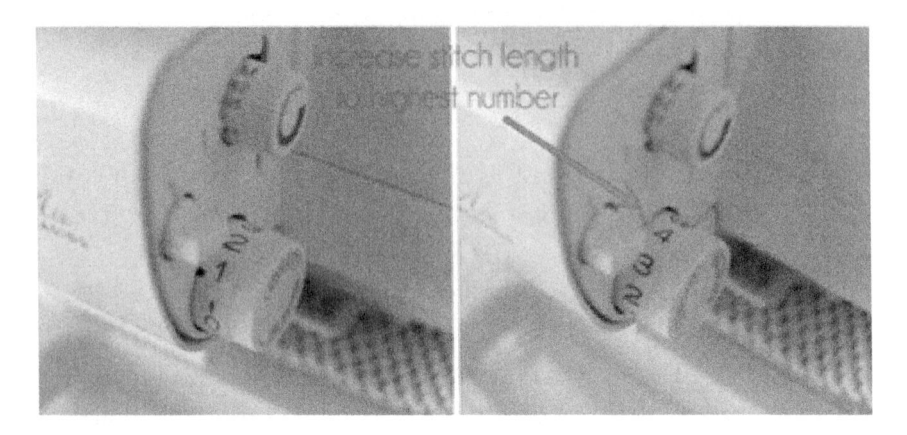

Step 3

Start to stitch along the raw edge of the fabric. You will notice some gatherings on your fabric as you continue to serge.

Step 4

Near the edge of the fabric, put your needle underneath the two parallel needle threads. Do not touch the looper threads otherwise, they will knot if you touch them.

Step 5

Pull the needle threads from the chain of threads as shown below. Make sure the threads don't get tangled. If done correctly, it will be easy to slip out.

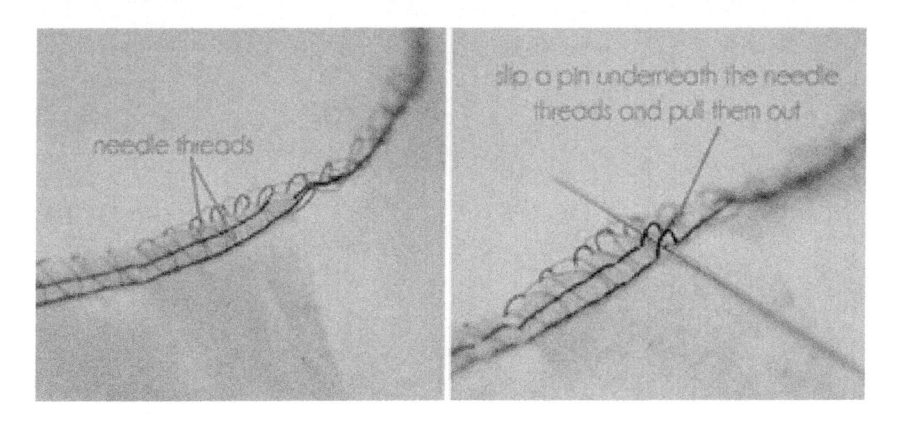

Then pull the two-needle threads in order to start gathering your fabric.

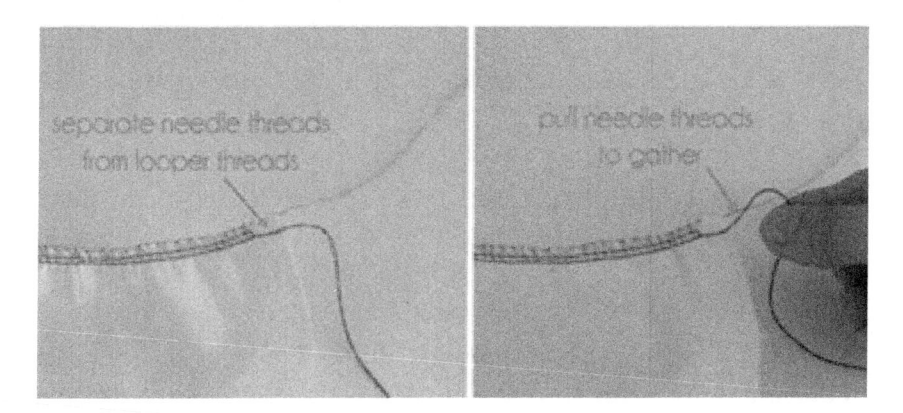

Step 6

Now you can go ahead and make gathers to your fabric. You will not have any stray threads that end up on the outside of your ruffled or gathered fabric.

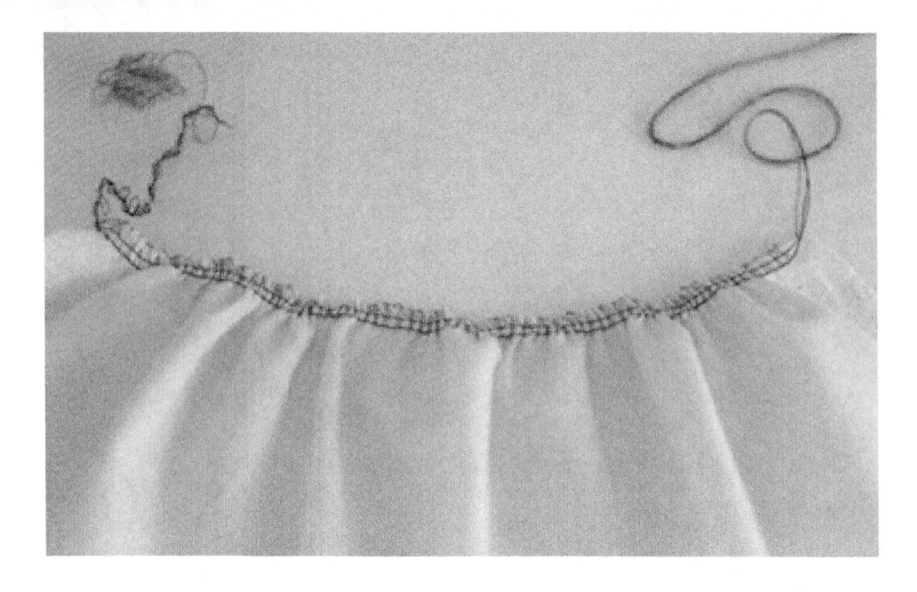

With these easy steps, you can easily serge your way to a great gathered project!

Tips for using a gathering foot

When using a gathering foot, it is difficult to control the length of the finished fabric unlike when using traditional gathering methods. You can solve this by cutting the fabric longer than the required size then trim the excess fabric after gathering. With this, you don't have to worry about how to get the perfect stitch length and tension.

Alternatively, you can use a test strip about 10 inches and then sew gathering stitches on it. Measure your new fabric length after the stitch. If the remaining length is 5 inches then you have 2:1 gather. Continue to adjust the stitch length and tension until you obtain the perfect ratio.

When sewing, ensure the flat fabric has the right side facing up and the fabric that needs to be gathered should have the wrong side facing up. That is, the garment and the ruffle must have the right sides together.

When gathering using a serger machine, you don't need a special foot tool or any attachments. All you have to do is adjust the stitch length and change the setting to a differential feeding system.

Chapter Summary

A gathering foot can help you to gather a piece of cloth or allow you to join a flat piece of cloth on the gathered fabric all at once. This saves you and gives you neat gathers.

With a perfect stitch length to tension ratio, you will be able to create gathers on your garment. A tight stitch is a result of having a long stitch length and a higher tension.

You can also create shirr gathers using an elastic thread to create rows of stitches. Although you can use a shirring foot, gathering foot also helps you create great projects with shirring effects.

Alternatively, you can use a serger machine to create your gathers. The serger is faster than the sewing machine. Once you know to use the serger, you will never go back to your normal sewing machine.

In the next chapter, you will learn about serger maintenance.

Chapter Three: Maintenance of Serger Machine

Maintenance of your serger machine is the most important thing you can do to extend the lifetime of your machine. Cleaning and oiling your serger sewing machine makes it run smoothly.

Like any other mechanical equipment, the quality of your serger performance is greatly influenced by regular care and maintenance. After every sewing project, you should remove any lint and bits of fabric remaining on the machine.

Image source: Evgeny Haritonov/Shutterstock

The lubricated area of the machine acts as a magnet that draws lint into the inside parts of your serger machine. The lint absorbs the oil leaving the moving parts to dry out. This affects the functioning of your machine and can shorten the machine life cycle.

Therefore, proper care will extend the lifetime of the machine as well as ensure your projects are perfectly made. For the sewing machine to function properly, it needs basic maintenance like cleaning, oiling, and lubricating it.

Serger requires a little bit of extra care because of its higher number of movable parts and serging speed.

All serger models come with a manual on how to clean them. You should go through the manual to learn how to clean and maintain your machine.

Having trouble with your machine?

When you're facing challenges with your serger machine, the general rule is to *clean it first*. Most of the problems you may be facing with your machine may be due to dust, lint, or pieces of threads that have collected from the working parts of your machine.

Leaving dust and lint to accumulate for long may affect the functioning of your machine. Simply brush them off after every use and you will have your machine run for a long time without any problems.

Sergers come with an attached soft nylon brush to clean the insides of the machine. Alternatively, you can use a narrow paintbrush to remove tint in the bobbin case, in the feed dog, and under the needle plate.

If there are pieces of thread or tint that you can't remove with the brush, then you can use tweezers to remove them.

If you leave lint to accumulate for a long time, it can be soaked with the oil or the lubricant and this will affect the operation of the machine. Once you remove this dirt you may notice the machine works properly and no further adjustments are needed.

Some of these instructions do not apply to all serger machines. Therefore, it is important to compare this guide with the specific procedures recommended to clean your machine by the manufacturer. For instance, a chain stitch machine or an electric machine that uses bearings packed with grease has specific instructions on how to clean, oil, and lubricate them.

Equipment and supplies

You need the following equipment and supplies to properly maintain your serger sewing machine.

- Small and a large screwdriver
- Small adjustable wrench
- Tweezers
- Needle holders
- Cake pan to soak parts in a cleaning fluid
- Small oil can for cleaning the fluid
- Paring knife/ pocket knife
- Cleaning brush (either nylon or narrow)
- Recommended sewing machine oil

- Small crochet hook
- Cleaning cloth
- Fabric to test stitches
- Sewing machine lubricant
- Can of cleaning solvent
- Flashlight
- Rubber gloves
- Old Newspapers
- Magnifying glass (optional)

Always check the machine's instruction manual of the recommended lubricant, cleaning solvent, and sewing machine oil. Use a cleaning solvent that doesn't flash a flame if temperatures go below 120° F. Carbon tetrachloride shouldn't be used because it is highly poisonous. You should never use gasoline because it is highly flammable.

Place newspapers on the floor or on the tabletop where you place your machine. You also need a flashlight for hard-to-see areas although this is optional.

General cleaning

Before you start cleaning your serger machine, you should assemble all the supplies and equipment you need. Unplug your machine and bring it to a well-lit room where you will do the cleaning.

If you want to do a full cleaning, unthread the machine, remove the needles, slide plate, and the presser foot. Some serger models allow you to remove the throat plate. Put all of them in a pan and add cleaning fluid to cover them. Leave them to soak and proceed with cleaning the other parts.

Make sure you note the position of each of the parts you remove and which side is supposed to be on the top. When unscrewing, make sure you put more pressure on the push and not on the twist. If a particular screw doesn't loosen up, then soak it with the cleaning fluid for a few minutes. The screwdriver blade size should be proportional to the slot in the screw. You should also use a wrench on the bolts and not pliers.

Open the serger doors to have access to the loopers. Take the soft nylon brush or the paintbrush and start cleaning the inside. Brush the area around the loopers and the feed dog to remove all the lint in the area. You can also use a brush that has some stiff bristles to push all the lint out. If there are threads sticking in some areas where the brush cannot reach, you can use tweezers to pull the threads.

After cleaning the looper, apply oil around that area using the manufacturer's recommended oil. In most cases, apply oil on the moving parts of the metal. One or two drops of oil are enough.

Clean the tension dials using a Perle cotton or a piece of embroidery floss. This will remove lint and threads left in the tension dial. If lint builds up around the tension dials, it will affect the accuracy of tension dial settings as well as interfere with stitch length and formation.

If your knife cut chewed edges instead of a clean-cut, then it is time to replace them. There are sergers that have only one blade while others have two: the upper blade and lower blade. Depending on the type of your machine, you can easily replace your knives. Make sure you return the knife to the precise position for it to work correctly. Alternatively, you can look for a serger technician to replace the knife for you.

After you're done cleaning and oiling the machine, screw back the presser foot, the stitch plate, and any other plate you removed. Replace the needle with a new one. You should always insert a new needle into your machine after cleaning it.

Wipe clean the outside of the serger to remove any fingerprints and thread your machine.

Oiling

Not all sergers require oiling so check the model manual to know whether to oil and after how long. The manual also has information on where to apply the oil and how often you should apply.

If your machines require oiling, there is a standard rule that states that the machine should be oiled after 8-10 hours of serging. You should also oil it whenever you hear a metallic scraping sound.

Changing needles

If you have bent or nicked a needle it may end up breaking or skipping some stitches while sewing. Bent needles can also cause the serger timing to go off, so you should change your needles more often.

Some manufacturers recommend changing the needles after every 8-10 hours of serging. Following some of these simple steps to keep your serger machine clean will increase the lifetime of your machine. You will never have any issues with the machine!

Chapter Summary

Maintenance of your serger machine is very important. Cleaning and lubricating the machine extends the machine's life and boosts the performance of your serger.

Different manufacturers have specific recommendations on how to take care of a particular model of the serger. Make sure to look at the recommendation before putting the above steps into practice.

Each model of the machine does recommend the type of oil to use while other brands don't need oiling. Therefore, read the instruction manual on what type of oil to use for each model of machine.

In the next chapter, you will learn how to make a baby blanket.

Chapter Four:
How To Make Baby Blanket

Learning how to make a baby blanket will give you great satisfaction. Baby Blankets are a more personal gift for the baby and the parent. It is the best gift any parent can give or receive. Making your own baby blankets is what makes them more special.

Image source: Kitch Bain/Shutterstock

Making a blanket to keep your little one warm gives you some sense of satisfaction. It is also a great gift to your loved ones!

Learning how to make baby blankets is a simple serging project for a beginner and it prepares you for making more basic serging projects.

There are various designs for homemade sewn baby blankets you can make for your loved ones. Some of these designs are simple and easy to use. Choose the design of your choice and make a great blanket for your baby.

If you're expecting your baby very soon, or someone you love is, then this simple project for making a baby blanket is for you. Let's get started.

Tools required

- 2 pieces of cloth
- Cutting mat
- Rotary cutter/ scissors
- Pins
- Thread
- Serger machine

Make sure to purchase fabrics designed specifically for baby clothing. In this project, we will use flannelette fabric. You can choose any other soft fabric but make sure it is made of breathable natural fiber and soft on the baby's skin.

In this tutorial, we are going to make a light baby blanket. If you want to make a heavyweight blanket, you can add an extra layer of flannel inside the blanket.

You can also wash the fabric before you start sewing. This will remove any chemical finishing left on the fabric that might irritate the baby. Some natural fabrics do shrink after washing them, so washing the fabric before sewing helps prevent further shrinkage.

Steps to follow

- Cut fabric to your desired size
- Pin the two pieces of the fabric together
- Sew stitches all around the blanket and leave an open space at the corner of the blanket.
- Turn the right way out
- Sew the open space

The beauty of making your own DIY project is to choose the features and details you want to be incorporated into your project. When it comes to choosing the size for your blanket, you can go for a size that suits you.

Step 1

Cut the two pieces of fabric based on your desired size. One-piece will be used for the front while the other piece will be for the back. You can sew round corners that look more professional than square corners. It is also easy to sew rounded corners.

You can use tins or other kitchen equipment to make round corners. Avoid using plates because they are too large.

Fold your fabric into quarters then cut the four-round corners at once. This ensures you have even corners. If you have a thick fabric, you can cut two layers at a time instead of 4 layers.

Step 2: Optional

Add embroidery to the top fabric. If you want to personalize the baby blanket, then you can do that at the front fabric. Make sure any stitching you're going to add or the trims are safe for your baby. You can also add applique, adorable little characters, and other patterns to make the blanket more attractive.

Step 3

Pin the two pieces of the fabric together and ensure the right sides face each other. Go ahead and stitch all four edges of the fabric using a 12mm seam allowance. Leave at least a 3-inch opening (7.5 cm) on one side of the fabric.

If you're using the square corners, then you will have to stop at every corner, lift the presser foot, and pivot to sew stitches on the next side. But if you're using rounded corners, the sewing will be continuous. No stopping and turning the fabric to sew the other side.

You can add more than one row of stitch to your blanket, you can have more rows to decorate the blanket. Alternatively, you can use different stitch options instead of using the regular straight stitch.

Step 4

Clip the curves of your blanket to reduce bulkiness and ensure you have a flat seam. Clipping ensures corners look neat and more professional when turned to the right side.

After clipping the blanket, it is time to turn the right way out via the 3 inch gap you left. Poke the corners of the blanket out. Do not use any sharp object to poke the corners.

Press the blanket to give it a great look and ensure the seams appear flat. Use an up and down motion when pressing rather than using the sliding method. Press also the seam allowance at the gap area.

Step 5

Topstitch around the edges of your baby blanket in order to close the gap. If different fabrics are used for both top and bottom, then you need to use matching colors for your top and bobbin.

Chapter Summary

Making a blanket for your baby doesn't have to take more than 20 minutes. With these few steps, you can easily make one for the new member of your family. Once you know how to make them, I am sure you would want to make them a gift too!

You can personalize the blanket by adding embroidery letters and other patterns of your choice. Make sure any additional embroidery you do on the blanket is safe for your baby.

Baby items use a small amount of fabric, so you can keep practicing by coming up with different designs like the colorful bunny blanket, adding patchwork pieces like you would on a quilt and a lovely binding border.

There are different options to choose from, keep practicing and you will be able to make more DIY projects.

In the next chapter, you will learn how to make your own pillow covers.

Chapter Five:
How To Make Your Own Pillow Covers

Pillow covers are a great accessory to add glam to your home. They are easy to make and any beginner can make one in less than ten minutes.

You can also make zippered pillow covers instead of using hem tape that will leave the pillows with a bulging seam.

Do not be afraid to take the challenge and make your own pillow covers. Some people are also afraid of sewing zippers in their projects. With this tutorial, you will find it is much easier than you think. So adding zippers doesn't have to be scary anymore.

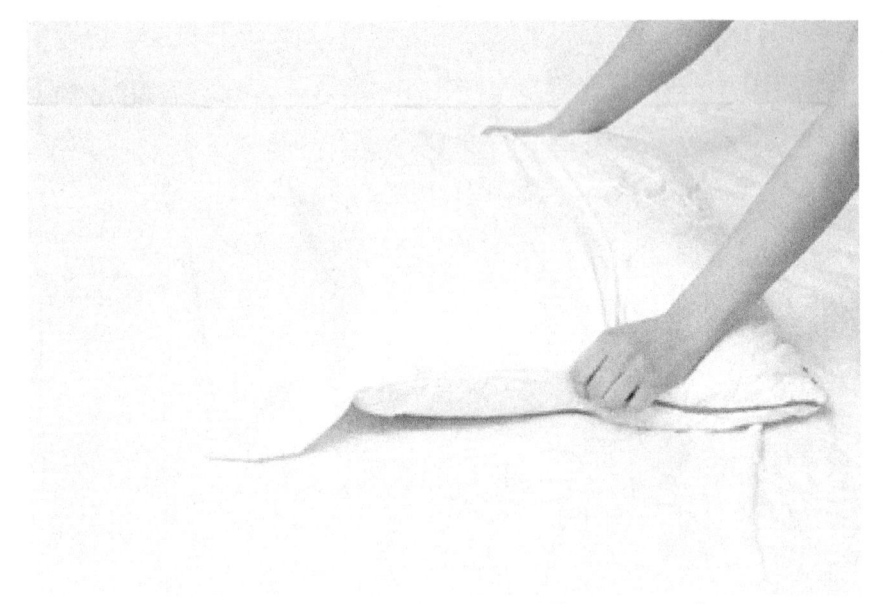

Image source: FotoDuets/Shutterstock

It's time to learn how to make your own pillow covers, you can even personalize them based on your preferences. After learning these simple steps, you will never spend money again buying pillow covers.

Choosing your own fabric that freshens up your living space is something you're going to do more often. Once you learn how to make one, you will keep making more pillow covers with different colors and patterns for your home.

So how do you make the pillow covers? Follow these step-by-step guides to make your own.

Required materials

- Half yard of fabric: Home décor fabric is the best for making the pillow covers because the material is thicker and it holds its shape nicely. You will need two pillow cut pieces of the same dimensions as that of the pillow insert.

- Invisible zip: Make it to be about 4 to 5 inches. Always make sure the zipper is shorter than the bottom edge of your pillow.

- Pillow insert: You can have 16 inch pillows that will look good on your sofa.

- Matching thread: Same color with the fabric you're sewing.

- Scissors or rotary cutter to make cuts perfect.

- Pins: To hold the pieces together.

- Tailor's chalk: To mark the areas where you want to cut the fabric.

- Measuring tape: To measure accurate size required to make the pillow covers.

Steps to make pillow covers

Step 1

Fold the fabric into half and lay the fabric on a flat surface. Use the measuring tape to mark 8 inches and 16 inch wide fabric. Cut the two pieces of fabric.

The size of the fabric to cut depends on the size of the pillow inserts. Make sure to cut the same size for the pillow cover to make the cushion look fuller.

Step 2

Stitch the zip by folding one side of the 8 inch fabric and pin the zip on the underside of the fabric. Place the fabric under the presser foot and remove the pin and start serging. If you have more than one pin, you can remove them as you continue serging.

If you cannot control the serging speed, you can use masking tape to hold the zip in place while serging instead of the pins.

Once you have stitched the zip on one piece of the fabric, do the same to the remaining piece of the fabric and ensure the zip is closed.

Trim any excess fabric and sewing the zippers.

Step 3

Stitch the other sides of the pillow covers. Once you have stitched the zip on both sides of the fabric, put the perpendicular sides together with the right side face each other and pin the seam line.

Place the fabric underneath the presser foot and start stitching following the seam line. Remove the pins as you continue stitching. Do the same to the other perpendicular side.

Step 4

Pin the remaining bottom side of the fabric. Open the zip then stitch the bottom side following the seam line. Remove the pin as you continue stitching to avoid breaking the needles or creating another problem for the machine.

Step 5

Serge the edges of the pillow to avoid coming off although you have zippered pillow covers that make it possible to take them off and wash. So if you need them to last, you have to finish the edges of the pillow cover.

Serge all the edges and trim any excess fabric using your serger machine. Adding finishing to the edges prevents them from fraying and you can wash the pillow covers as many times as you want without any worry.

Step 6

Turn the pillow cover with the right side out and press the edges to make the pillow cover look neat. Now you can add the pillow insert and zip up to enjoy your new pillow.

Chapter Summary

Making your zippered pillow covers doesn't have to be scary. With these few steps, you can make your own pillow cover. You can be more creative and add more decorative designs to the pillow covers to glam your sofa.

You can also make pillow covers with different colors to match your home color theme. Personalizing these pillow covers for your home will bring you the greatest satisfaction.

So go ahead and practice more and become a pro in making the pillow covers. You can also make them as a gift to your loved ones.

In the next chapter, you will learn how to make a drawstring bag using a serger machine.

Chapter Six:
How to Make Drawstring Bag Using Serger Machine

Drawstring bags are a great accessory and they are easy to make. A drawstring bag can be used for holding small items together, separating your clothes and shoes in a suitcase while traveling, carrying it as a picnic bag, etc. You can customize the size of the drawstring based on your personal preferences.

Image source: xiaorui/Shutterstock

If you have some scraps left, you can cut enough material and make a drawstring bag for yourself.

They are very easy to make and can act as a perfect size for a little gift bag. You will find it much faster to sew these little bags using your overlock machine. Learning to make these drawstring bags can help organize all your smaller tools in a simple manner. You can also give them as a gift during baby showers or birthday parties.

What are drawstring bags?

A drawstring is an open-top bag secured with a drawstring closure that runs around the top of the bag. The drawstring closure acts as the handle to carry the bag by your hands or use it as a shoulder sling to carry the bag as a backpack.

These bags have easy accessibility and are lightweight making them suitable for carrying a small number of supplies. They are mainly designed for your daily use and can help you organize with ease.

You can bring them with you when going to parties, games, the beach, or the gym. Its unique designs allow you to bring them with you on a wide range of occasions. Some of the classy designs serve as a trendy fashion accessory for the younger generation.

Let's learn how you can make one for yourself.

Materials required

- Cotton fabric, at least 10-inch squares
- 2 strips of material, the same width as your bag
- 1 yard of ⅛ inch ribbon cut into half
- 3 spools of matching serger thread
- Large-eye needle or bodkin to thread ribbon

- Serger machine with a standard Presser foot

Steps to make the drawstring bag

Step 1

Prepare the fabric

Cut two strips of the fabric with the same width as your bag and 2 inches/50mm tall to make the bag casing. Fold the ends of the two casing pieces at ½ inch/10mm.

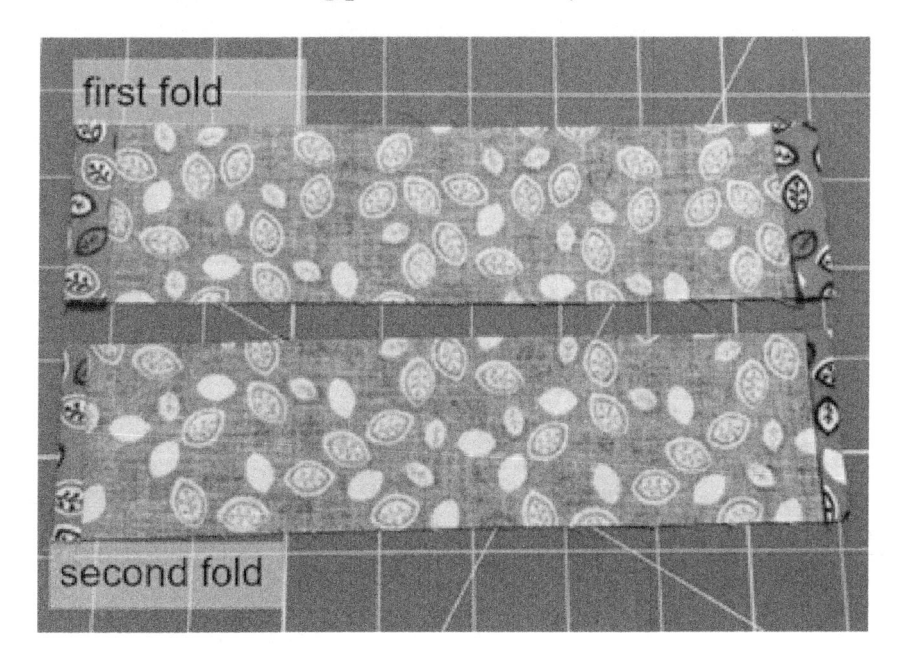

Step 2

Fold the raw edge again under itself and press the fold. Do the same on the other piece of casing. Serge the folded edges of the casing and make sure you serge on all the layers to prevent fraying of the edges.

Step 3

Fold the strips into half and press them hard enough to leave a crease.

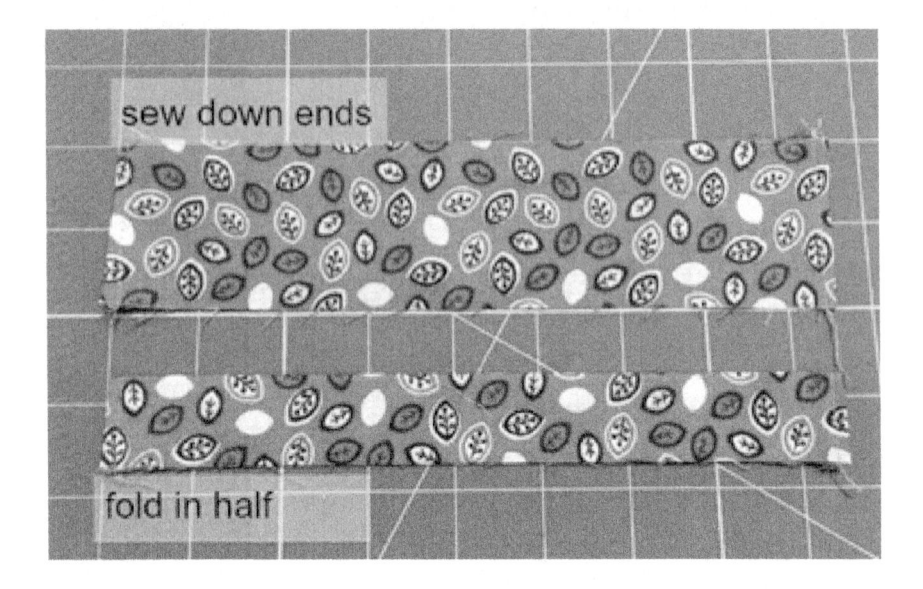

Step 4

Fold a piece of the casing strip and one piece of cotton fabric into half and press hard enough to leave a crease.

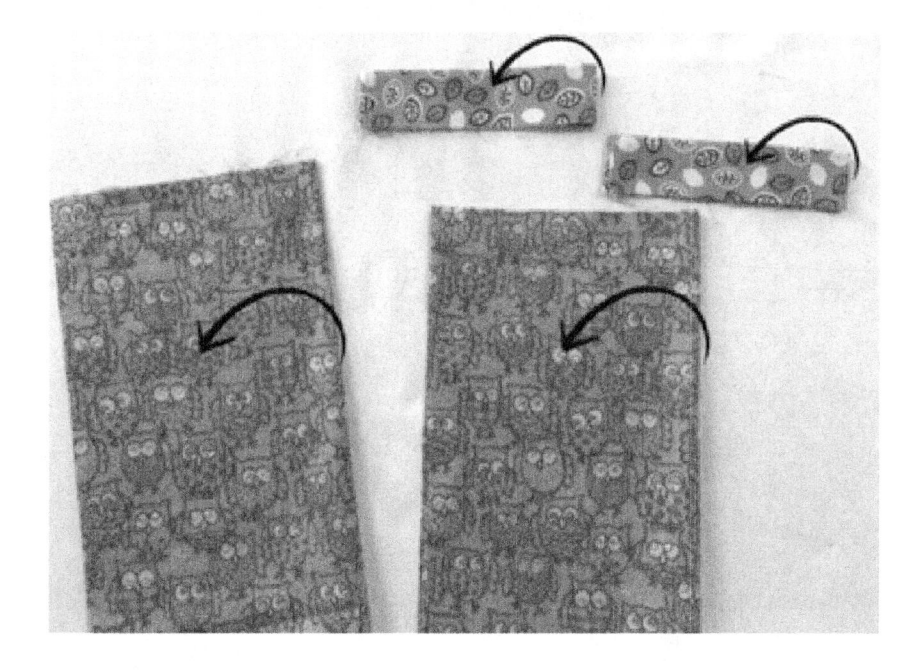

Step 5

Place the raw edges of the casing strip on the right side of one piece of the cotton fabric. Line the casing strip at the top edge of the bag fabric. Pin the pieces together to keep them in place. Do the same to the other piece of fabric and casing strip.

Lift your presser foot and place the attached piece of fabric underneath it to serge. Lower the foot and start serging the bag and the strip together. Reduce your serging speed so that you can remove the pins holding the fabric as you continue serging using a 6mm seam allowance.

Step 6

Press the casing strip and seam allowance to make the seams neat. Add a topstitch at the front to strengthen your bag and at the same time to catch the seam allowance on the underside.

Step 7

Place the two bag pieces together with the right sides facing each other. Serge around the two sides of the bag and the bottom side using a 6mm seam allowance. You can choose a different seam size, you don't have to stick to a 6mm seam.

Step 8

Turn right side out and press the edges.

Now you can feed the ribbon into the casing of the bag. Use the large needle or the bodkin to insert the ribbon in the casing. You can start inserting the bodkin on any side. You can start on the right side.

Step 9

When you get into the gap in the casing, jump it and continue to insert the bodkin into the other casing piece. Bring out the bodkin at the end of your bottom casing. Tie both ends of the ribbon together.

Use the same step to feed the second ribbon into the casing starting in the opposite direction of the first ribbon (left side).

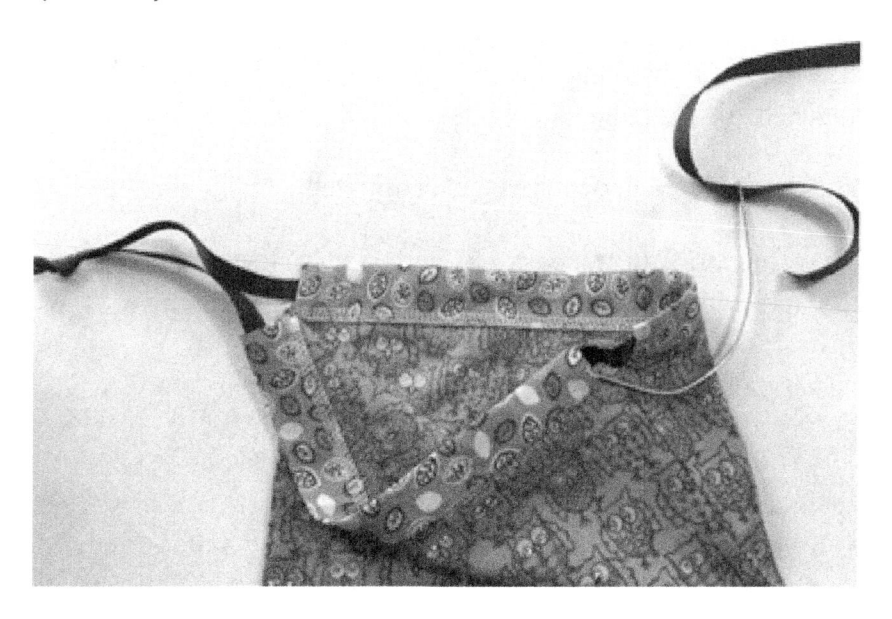

Step 10

Tie the two ribbon pieces together. To prevent unraveling on the cut ends of the ribbon, you can apply a fray check.

Now your drawstring bag is ready for your use. Once you put your items in the bag, you can pull the ribbons on both sides to close it.

When making the ribbon, make sure to choose a thread that matches your fabric color. You can also use the same fabric for the casing and the bag.

If you want to make your drawstring bag more attractive, you can use a box for the bottom corner or add patch pockets to the bag to hold a few more items. There are different ways you can make your drawstring bag. You can choose among different designs that appeal to your eyes and go ahead to make the drawstring.

Making box bottom drawstring bag

A box bottom drawstring bag is a type of string bag that sits up on its own. If you want to package a gift, using a drawstring with a box bottom will look classy and esthetically appealing.

You can easily customize a drawstring based on shape, design, size, and even height. The best drawstring is one with a stable bottom to allow you to place it on any flat surface.

Let's see how you can make your own packaging gift with a stable bottom!

Requirements

- Two pieces of fabric each measuring 10 inches * 9 inches
- Two pieces of the lining, 10 inches * 9 inches
- Two pieces of ribbon or string 28 inches
- Matching thread
- Safety Pin

Step 1

Hold the two pieces together with the right sides facing each other and serge around the fabric edges within a 0.25 inch seam allowance. Leave the top side open and a gap on either of the sides to add the drawstring.

A gap approximately 1-inch wide is enough and should be 2.5 inch from the top. Since you're going to use the drawstring more often, it's good to backstitch the gap area. If your fabric has some stripes, consider lining them up to give a cleaner look.

Step 2

Put the two pieces of lining together with the right side facing each other. Stitch around the sides of the lining including the bottom but leave the top open. No need to leave gaps on the lining.

Press the seams.

Step 3

After serging around on the main fabric and lining, you're ready to make the box corners. To do this, a special stitch is required on the left corner and right corner of your bag.

Let's start with the left corner. You can decide which corner you want to start with.

Start by lining up the bottom seam together with the side seam and hard press such that the material appears flat and at 90 degrees.

Use a ruler to draw a straight line, using the tailor's chalk or fabric pencil, where the legs of the triangles are at 3 inches.

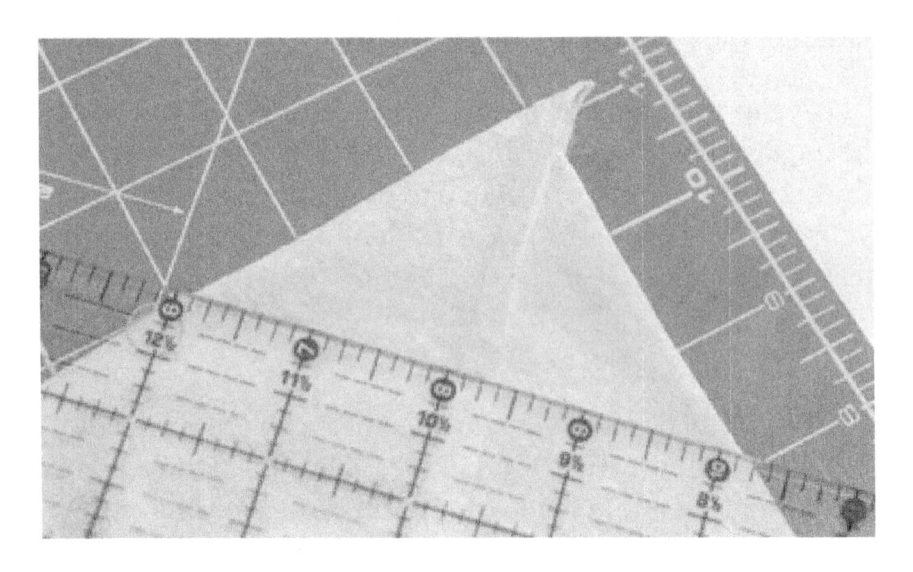

Step 4

The line drawn is the hypotenuse of the triangle. Draw the line on both sides of the bag and on top of the line, sew a straight stitch.

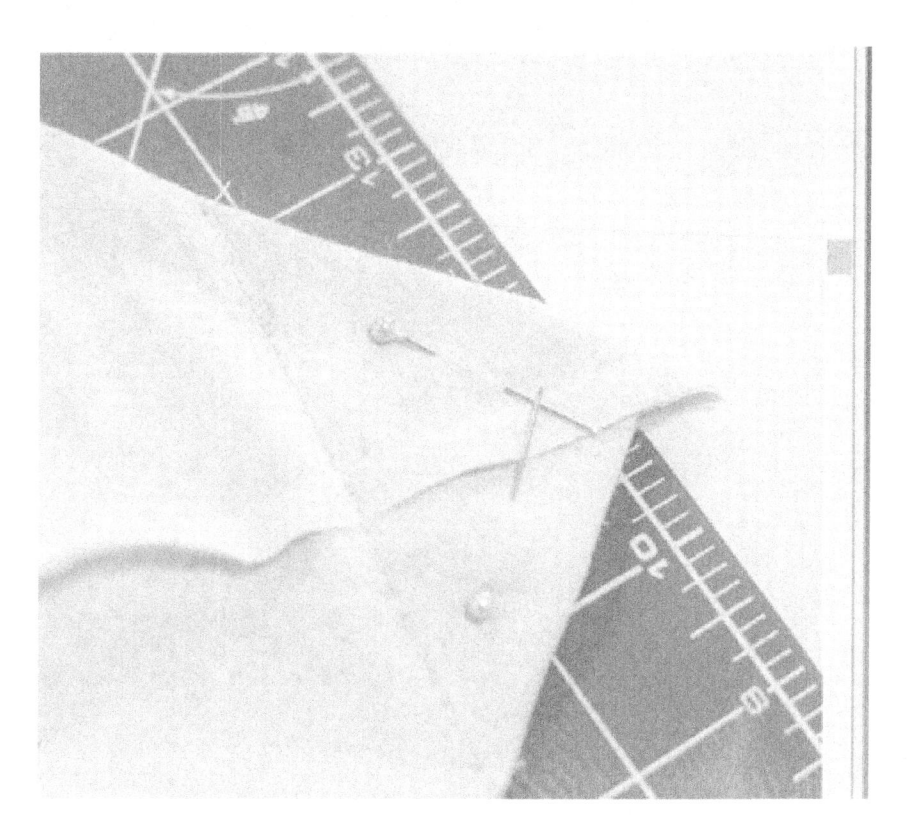

Step 5

Cut the corners of the fabric while leaving at least 1.8 inches of the seam allowance.

Repeat the same process on the right corner of the bag. Draw the line, stitch, and clip both sides of the fabric

Step 6

Turn the main fabric to have the right side while the lining should have the right side out and put the lining inside of the main fabric.

Step 7

Ensure the side seams on both fabrics match and pin them in place.

Step 8

Leave a gap about 2 inches wide so that you can turn the main fabric right side out.

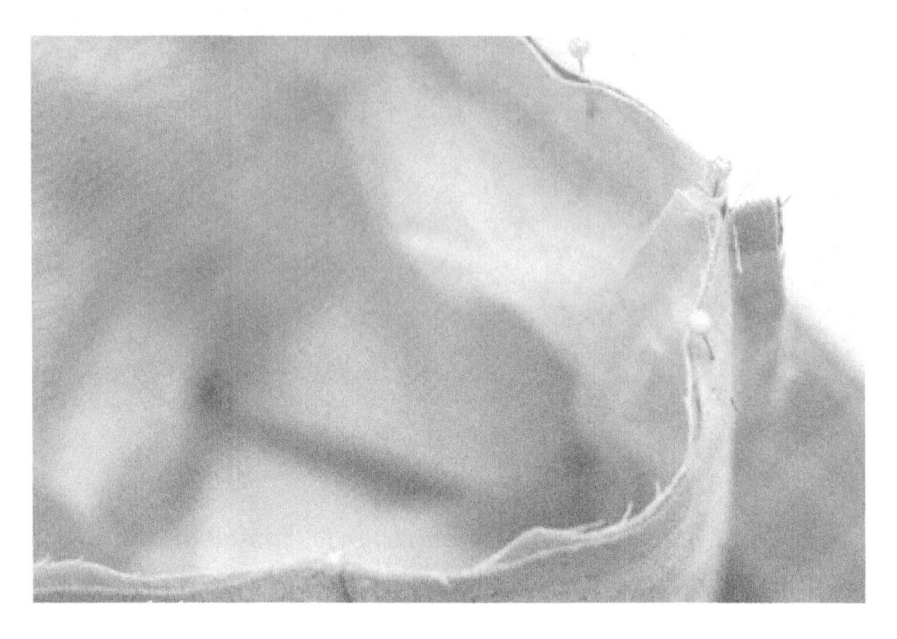

Step 9

Stitch on top of your bag leaving 0.25 inch seam allowance

Now turn the main fabric right side out via the gap. This will leave the main fabric and the lining facing out.

Step 10

Now push the lining inside your main fabric and hard press at the top where the main fabric meets the lining so as to have a smooth and clean edge.

Step 11

Use a ⅛ inch seam allowance to stitch around your bag and close up the gap.

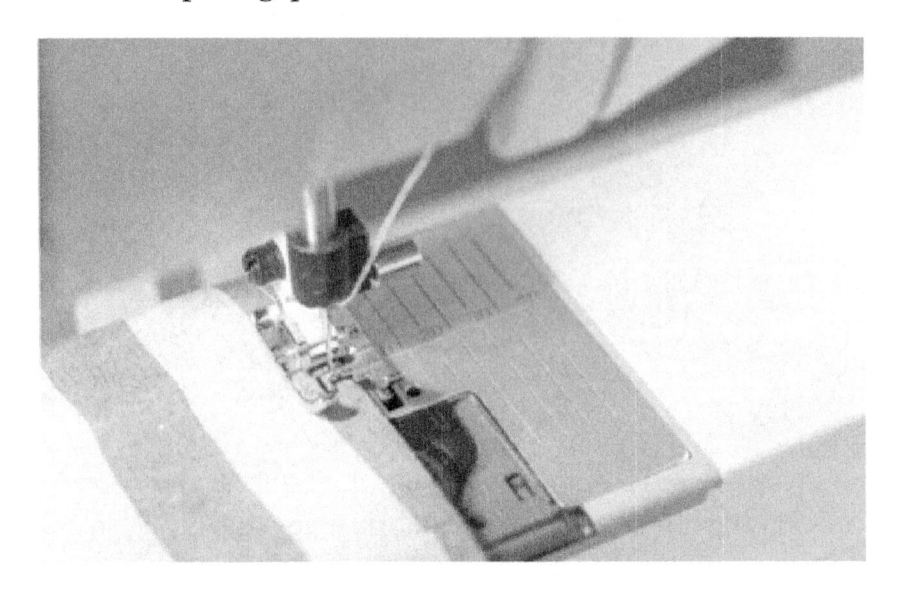

Step 12

Use your drawing chalk to draw two lines above and below the drawstring gap on the sides of the bag to create a casing.

Stitch at the top of the lines all around the bag. If you want a cleaner start and finish of the stitches, you can start stitching at the seam.

Step 13

Now it's time to add the ribbon or a piece of twine to make your drawstring. Take one piece of twine and loosely tie it to a safety pin. You can use a large needle or bodkin to do this.

Step 14

Feed the safety pin through one of the drawstring gaps and feed it through the casing. When you reach the gap on the other side, skip it and continue to feed the safety pin to the casing. The twine/ribbon should enter and exit out of the gap on the same side.

Step 15

Tie a knot on the two ends of the twine. Repeat the same process to the second gap on the other side of the bag. When the twine comes out at the other end, take the two ends and tie them together.

You can now pull your strings to form your drawstring bag.

Your bottom looks stable and you can place the bag on any flat surface after filling your goodies inside.

In our second example, we have created the casing in the main fabric compared to having an extra fabric for the casing. Therefore, you don't have to limit yourself. You can go for a simple drawstring bag or go for classy designs with box bottoms. There's no excuse not to make your own drawstring bag.

You can also make a drawstring bag to carry on your back. Once, you have been able to successfully do the two examples, you can make a drawstring of any shape.

Chapter Summary

Drawstrings bags have become very popular due to their weight-bearing capacity. Depending on the design and size, they have a wide array of uses. The younger generation use them as trendy fashion bags to carry around or use them to sort out and store various accessories at home.

Depending on the uses of the bag, you can make a size suitable for your needs. With the above simple steps, you can make a drawstring for any occasion and use. They don't require a large amount of fabric so if you have some fabric left after a sewing project, you can use the remaining to make the drawstring bag.

You can make a smaller size drawstring with a box bottom to use as a packaging gift.

In the next chapter, you will learn how to make a dust cover for your serger machine.

Chapter Seven:
Dust Cover For A Serger Machine

A dust cover for your serger machine is essential. If you are in an environment with a lot of dust, you need to get a dust cover for your serger machine to extend its lifetime. When not using the machine you should cover it. This not only keeps your machine free from dust, it adds some color to the sewing room!

If you have children, I am sure you don't want any needle-related accidents on their little fingers. Sometimes children can mess up the threading and settings of your machine especially if you have taken a break from your sewing project. In such situations, I'm sure you don't want to come right back to a total mess. A simple cover goes a long way to shield from dust and little fingers away.

Sergers come in different shapes and designs, therefore, having a custom made dust cover gives you more satisfaction compared to ready-made dust covers available on the market.

In this tutorial, you will learn step-by-step procedures on how to make your own dust cover. It is easy, quick, and more functional than some dust covers in the market. To make it more unique, we will add a pocket to store notions and other serger accessories.

Let's have some fun making a dust cover for your machine.

Requirements

- 1 yard of outer fabric 1
- 1 yard of fabric 2
- Pencil
- Scissors
- Matching thread
- Pins
- 1 yard of folded Bias tape
- Fusible fleece
- Tape measure
- Iron and ironing board
- Serger machine

If you need a quilted dust cover that covers your machine from front to back using two side pieces, you have to measure your machine to get the right dimensions.

How to make a dust cover

Step 1: Taking measurements

Measure the front of your machine in the base area. That is the widest part of the machine. If your machine has a wheel, you need to add that to your measurement. Then add an extra 1 inch to 1.5 inch for seam allowance.

It is better to have a loose dust cover than a tight one that is hard to fit your machine in. The extra inches will give you plenty of room.

The next measurement you should take is across the front going all the way to the back. Start from the table and go up the front of your machine up to the thread tree and across the back to the table at the back.

You will notice the measurements are in a slanting position. Depending on the type of machine, you can adjust your tape measure to have straight measurements.

Measure the width of your machine. You need to measure the height of the machine. Do that from the table to the top.

If you use estimates, the cover may turn out extra-large. Don't worry, if the cover turns out to be too big, you can always trim it to get the right size for your machine.

Based on your measurements, you can cut the fabric into squares, rectangles, or rectangles with rounded top corners.

Step 2: Creating pattern pieces

After taking the measurements, the first pattern piece you're going to make is the giant rectangle from the two measurements you took on your machine. That is the base length at the front and the measure from the front going across the back.

The next pattern piece will be for the sides of the machine (width*height). Curve the edges at the top of the fabric.

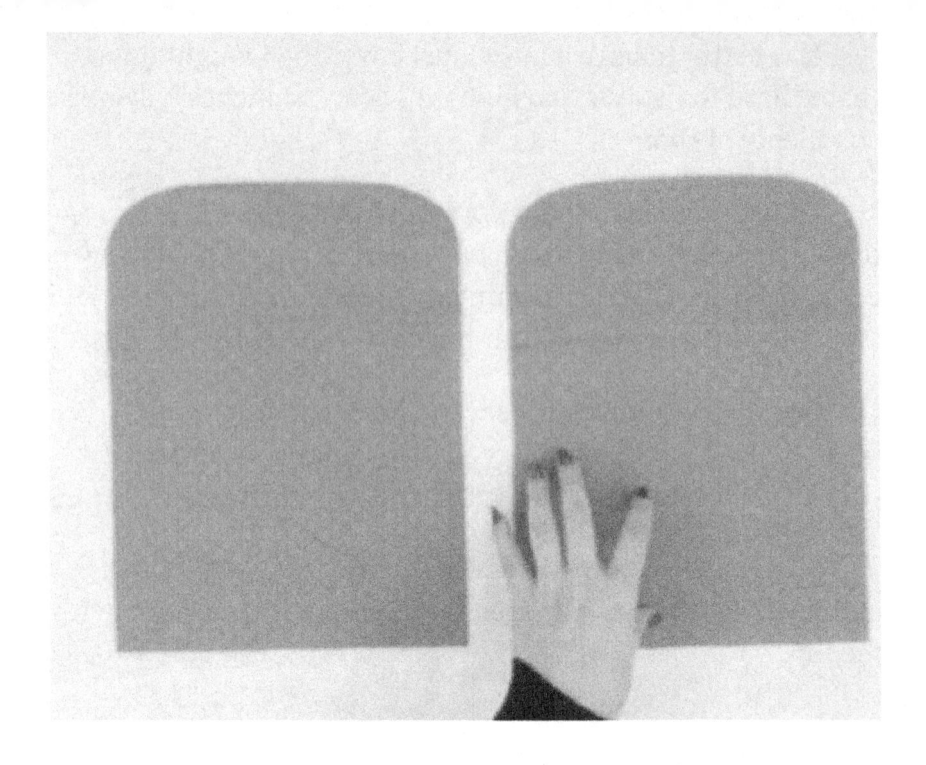

Now you have two patterns created: The main pattern and the side pattern.

You can add a pocket to your dust cover, although this is an option. Use the same width of the main pattern to make a pocket pattern. You only need to decide how high you need the pocket to be on the front of the machine. In this case, I used 5 inches. After cutting the pattern, you'll see it has a rectangle shape.

Step 3: Cutting the fabric

Now we have three patterns we're going to use to cut the fabric. On the main pattern, we will use the pattern to cut 1 piece from the outer fabric 1, 1 piece from fabric 2, and 1 piece from fusible fleece.

Using the side pattern, cut 2 pieces from the outer fabric 1, 2 pieces from fabric 2, and 2 pieces from fusible fleece.

Using the pocket pattern, cut the fabric you want to use for your pocket. You can decide to use the outer fabric 1 or fabric 2. Let's use fabric 2 to make the pockets.

Step 4

Apply the fusible fleece to the wrong side of the main fabric and on the two pieces of the side fabric. Press the two pieces together using your iron.

For better results, you can cover the fabrics with a piece of light material and spray it with your spray bottle. Then place the iron on top of the material to press them together.

Do not iron, only place your iron on top of the fabric at different spots to make sure the fleece doesn't come out of the attached fabric.

Be careful not to shift the fleece when covering with the piece of material.

Do the same to all three pieces of fabric. Make sure the fleece is applied on the wrong side of the fabrics.

it's fusible fleece not webbing

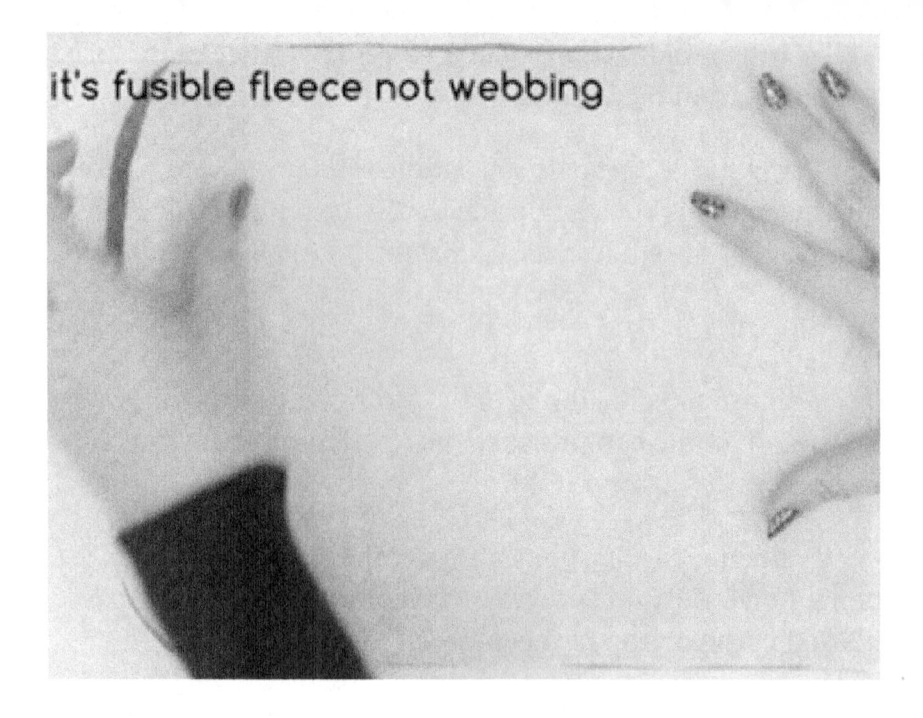

Step 5

Pin the two side pieces of fabric 2 into the long edge of the main fabric. Place the main fabric with the right side up such that it faces the right side of the side fabric.

Line the width of the main fabric with the width of the side fabric and pin the two fabrics on the edges.

Step 6

The curve length should line up with the length of the main fabric. When you get to the curve area, lift the fabric, and continue pinning the curve at the straight long edge of the main fabric going up to the other side.

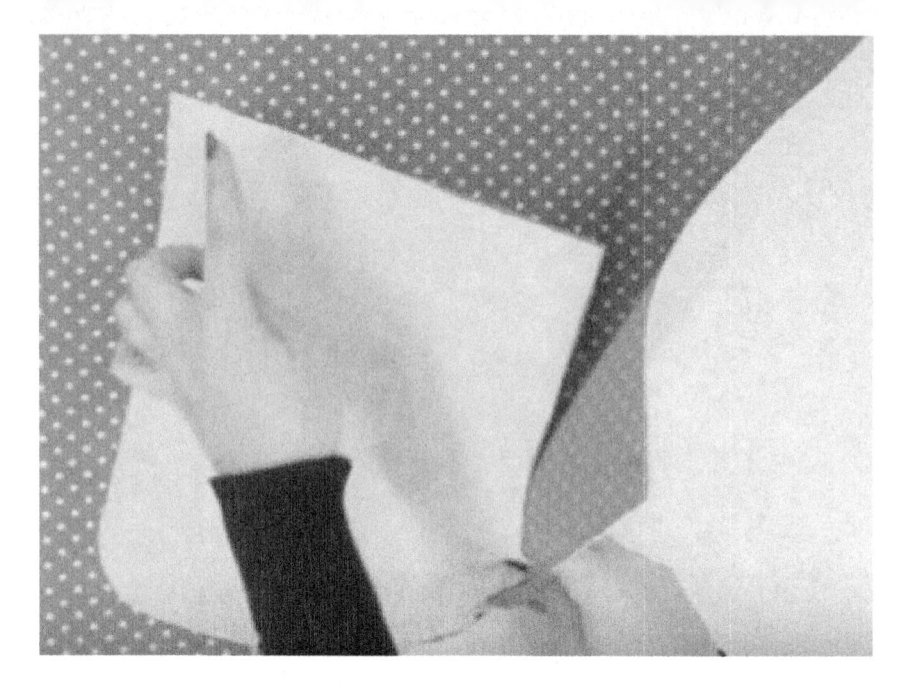

Step 7

After pinning, you will have something like this:

Step 8

Now pin the remaining piece of side fabric 2 on the other side of the main fabric using the same process.

Step 9

Stitching your fabrics together. Use ¼ inch seam allowance to stitch the pieces together. When you get around the curves slow your sewing speed and smoothen the fabric to avoid any wrinkles. Put the needle down and then lift the presser foot, adjust the fabric, and bring the presser foot down.

Continue stitching around the curve and then adjust the fabric again to have a smooth finished stitch. Be careful not to stitch on the pins, you can remove the pins as you continue stitching.

Stitch the other piece of side fabric on the other side of the main fabric.

Step 10

Stitch the side pocket to the fabric. Take the cut fabric and fold it into half width-wise. Press at the center to have a crease.

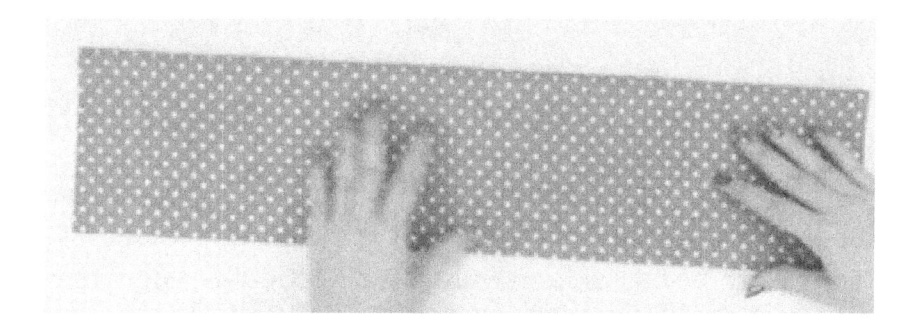

Step 11

Place the bias tape on the side with the crease. Pin it up to the end of the fabric. Since both sides are the same, it doesn't matter which side you pin the bias tape on.

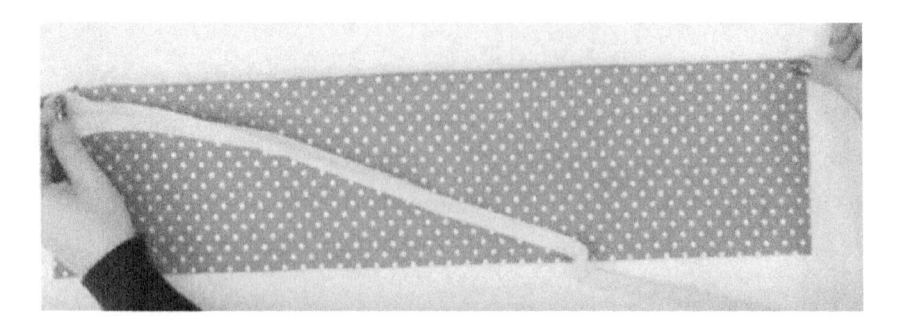

Step 12

At your machine, sew right at the edges of the crease. Use a regular stitch for this and don't forget to backstitch at both ends.

Step 13

Now take the bias tape and fold it over to the other side.

The edges of bias tape should cover the stitches you have made. Then sew the topstitch on the bias tape that catches the bias on the backside. Sew the stitch around the edges of the bias tape. Make sure you're using a matching color.

Step 14

Take your main piece of fabric 1 with the right side up so that you have your width on the downside and then take your pocket fabric and place it on top so the edges match up.

Step 15

Pin the fabric together and stitch a temporary base stitch on all the sides. If you need an individual compartment on the fabric, use the fabric marker to draw separating straight lines on the pockets and then stitch them.

Step 16

Just like we did with fabric two, take the individual side pieces and pin them to the main fabric with the right side facing each other.

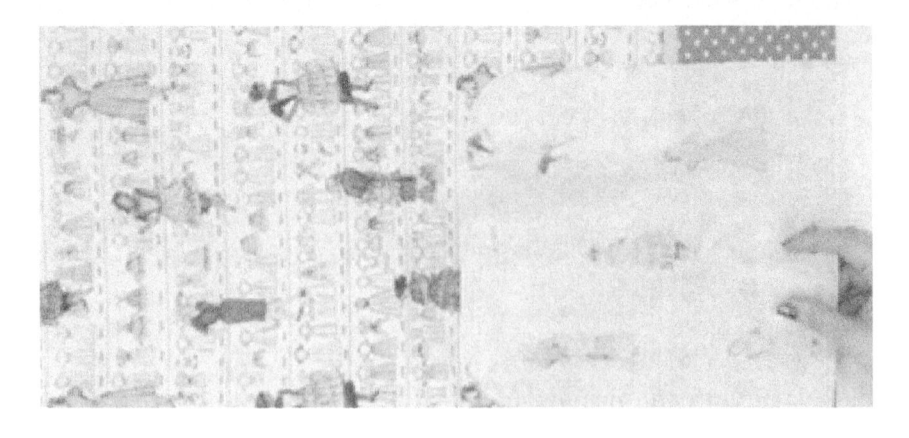

Lift the fabric and pin on the curves along the length of fabric 1.

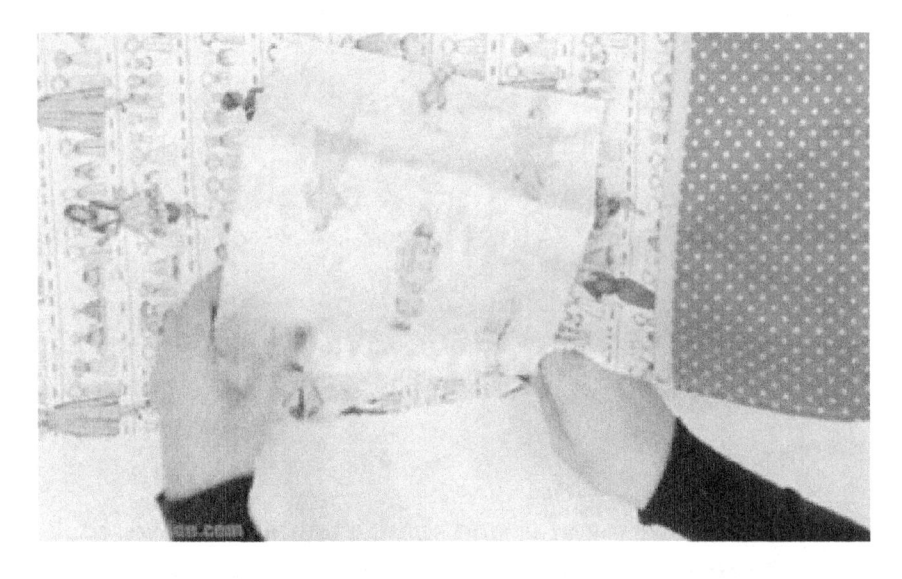

Flip the curves and pin around the full length. Do that for both sides of the fabric and stitch around the edges of both fabrics.

Step 17

Once you're done stitching fabric 1 and 2, try to press the seams open. Flip fabric 1 cover over fabric 2 covers so that the wrong sides are together. Match all the seams together and pin the raw edges together.

Use a bottom stitch to sew along all the bottom edges.

Step 18

Add the bias tape to finish the raw edges at the bottom. Take your bias tape and line it with the bottom raw edges of fabric 1. Fold the tape at the beginning of the fabric and pin it. When you flip it over, you will have a folded edge. Pin all the way around until you get to the other fabric.

Step 19

After pinning, you have to stitch on the crease. When you're done stitching, fold and flip the tap over to the wrong side of the fabric. Add a topstitch that catches the bias tape at the backside.

Now you have your dust cover for your serger machine. With this cover, there are no raw edges exposed and you can enjoy putting it on your machine. Now go ahead and make a dust cover for your machine.

Chapter Summary

Serger machines collect a lot of dust when not being used. Therefore, you need a dust cover to prevent dust from accumulating in your machine since it will have a negative impact on the long-run and functioning of the machine.

Keeping dust away ensures your machine operates smoothly. Some machines come with a plastic cover that isn't aesthetically pleasing although it does serve its purpose. Instead of buying a dust cover, use these steps to make a simple dust cover for your machine.

Your preparation for the size, fabric, and all other requirements you need determines the success of your project. Get the fabric of your choice and practice making a dust cover for your machine.

In the next chapter, you will learn how to make Christmas stocking.

Chapter Eight: Christmas Stocking

Christmas is here and it's a good opportunity to make stockings for your children. Christmas stocking resembles a sock-shaped bag that is usually hung during Christmas Eve and Saint Nicholas day so that either Saint Nicholas, Santa Claus, or Father Christmas can fill them with gifts.

Image source: Valentina Proskurina/Shutterstock

These gifts are toys, coins, fruits, candy or other small items and they are usually referred to as stocking stuffers.

According to some traditions, especially in Western culture, children who behave badly will only receive a single piece of coal in their stocking. Children hang up Christmas stockings around their home because they believe that Father Christmas will fill it with gifts.

This is actually a tradition that originated from the life of Saint Nicholas who put gold coins in the stockings of three poor sisters. One night, the girls had hung their stockings over the fireplace to dry. Saint Nicholas knew their father wouldn't accept the gifts, so he secretly threw three bags of gold coins through the window. One bag landed on the stockings. Since then, children have been hanging up their stockings on Christmas Eve with the hope that they will find them filled with gifts when they wake up.

There are a lot of stores that sell a variety of Christmas stockings made of different sizes and styles. Today, there are a lot of homemade Christmas stockings. Creating your own Christmas stocking allows you to customize it for your family and friends. You can have the names of the family members sewn on the stocking so that Santa or Father Christmas will know who it belongs to.

So how do you make a Christmas stocking? Keep reading to learn the step-by-step procedure on how to create Christmas stockings for your loved ones. You can also give it as a gift to your friends and extended family.

Making your own custom made stocking is very easy and cheap. Following these easy steps, you can make as many stockings as you want.

Requirements

- Fabric of your choice. For example, Comfy Flannel, fleece, or cotton.
- Lining material
- Matching thread

- Scissors/ Rotary cutter or cutting mat
- Pins or clips
- Tailor's chalk or Pencil
- Iron and ironing board
- Serger machine

Step 1

Cut the fabric to make your stocking. Make sure you have enough fabric to cut two pieces for the front and back and another fabric to cut the two linings pieces. Cut the front and back pieces of 13 inch *15 inch.

If you're using an old Christmas stocking to create your pattern for the new one, you can lay the old stocking on newspaper or brown paper. With your pencil or chalk trace all around the stocking leaving about ½ inch spacing. Remove the stocking and cut the pattern out.

Use the cut pattern to cut the outer fabric and lining for your new stocking, both the front and back fabrics.

Step 2

Hold the two pieces together with the wrong sides facing each other. Pin the pieces together and cut the stocking shape.

Step 3

Put the wrong sides together then cut the two pieces of stocking shapes for your outer fabric and the inner lining pieces. Ensure the toes are in the same direction as you cut the fabric. Matching the fabric on the wrong sides together ensures you cut stocking pieces that face both directions.

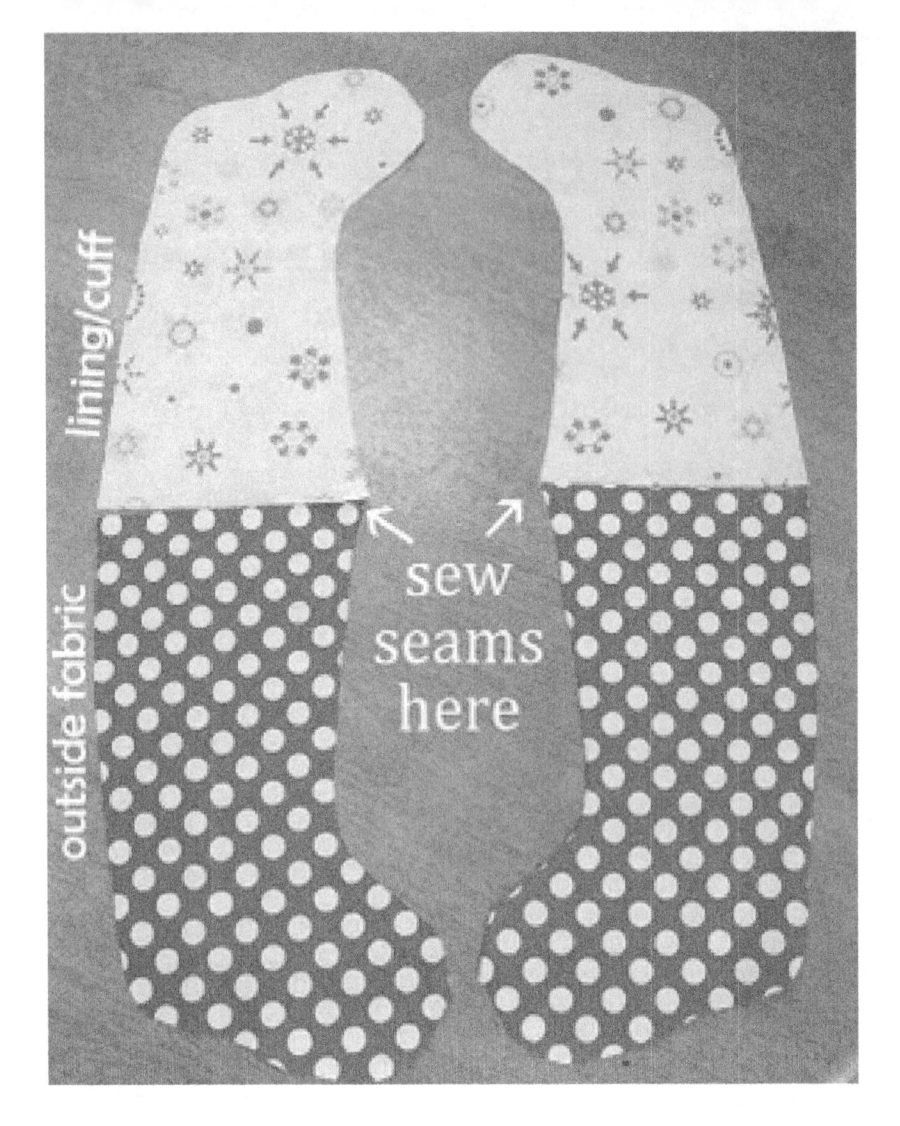

Step 4

Line one piece of the outer fabric with one piece of lining fabric and toes facing the same direction. With the right sides of both the outer and inner lining facing each other, stitch the two pieces with a ¼ inch seam and leave some gap on the stocking to help you turn the right side out after you're done with sewing.

After sewing, open the two pieces and press the seams for both the front piece and the backside. You can also use the iron to smoothen the seams.

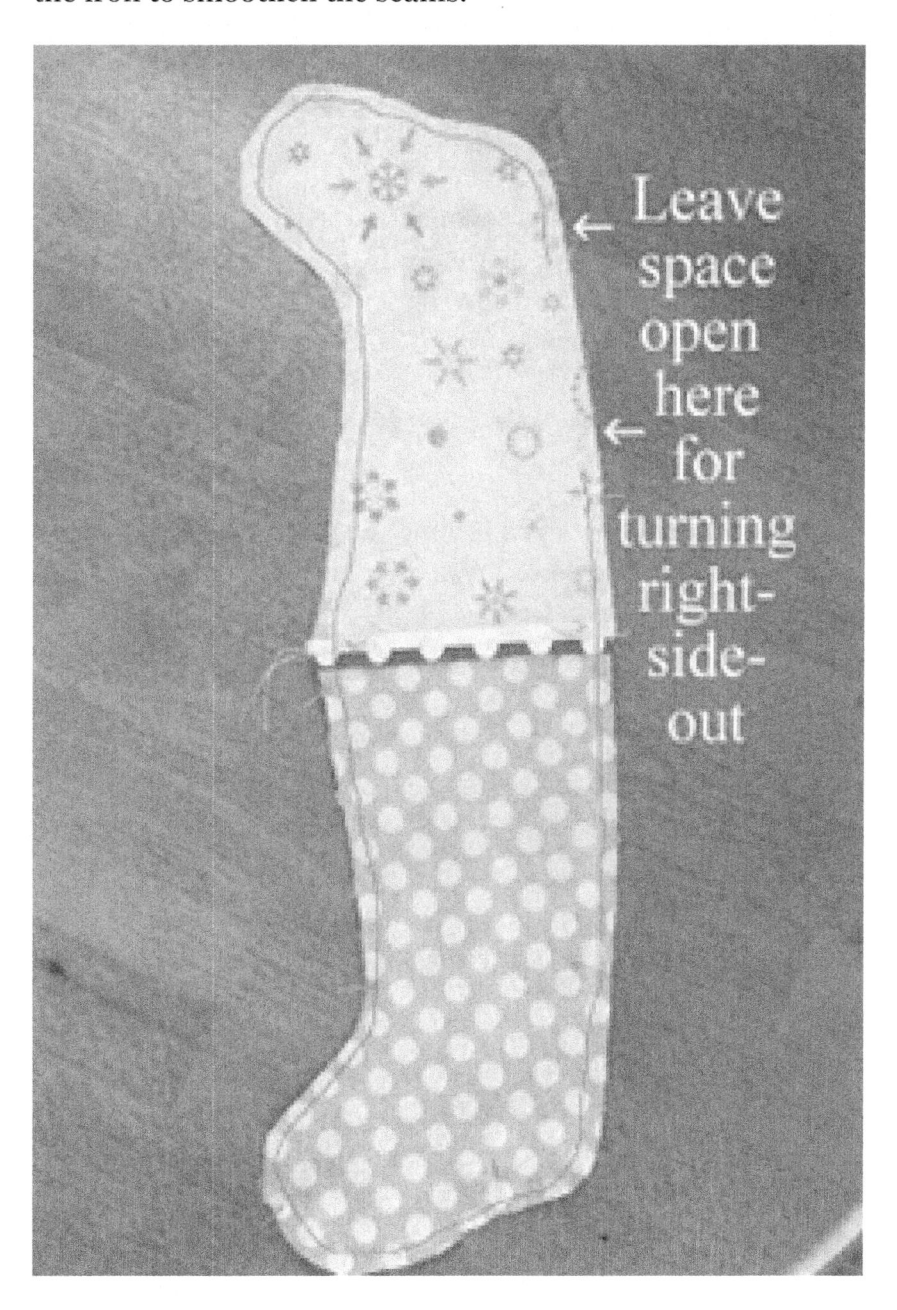

Step 5

Do the same to the other piece of the stocking. The right side out should face each other. The lining fabric should have the right side facing each other. Sew around the sides and leave a gap in the lining to turn the right side out. Ensure the center seams match each other.

You can use a ¼ inch seam allowance on the outside fabric and ⅜ inch lining on the lining fabric. This will make it easy to remove bulkiness on the seams of the lining fabric. Alternatively, you can use ¼ inch seams for both the outside fabric and the lining.

Step 6

Cut some notch curves around the toe curves. This will ensure your stocking looks neat when turned. Do not clip on the seam.

Step 7

Clip the lining fabric with the clips close to the seams to help remove bulkiness. Now turn the right side out and add topstitch to the stocking to close the gaps.

Turn stocking right-side out and topstitch opening closed.

Step 8

Press the seams to make the curves look neat. Tuck in the lining into the stocking and sew a top stitch around the edges of the opening to give it a more finished look.

Step 9

Fold the cuff down and add a decorative seam to make your stocking look more attractive. Although, this is optional. You can even use craft glue to add ric racks as shown below.

Step 10

Make a hanger for your Christmas stocking. Cut a rectangle piece of fabric and fold it in half to make the long sides touch each other. Press at the center of the fabric to create a middle crease.

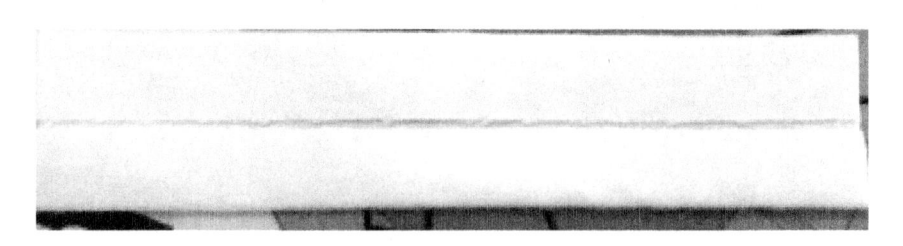

Open the rectangle. Make a fold at the raw edges of the fabric so as to meet the freshly created middle crease and press the fold.

Do the same on the lower opposite raw edge.

Step 11

Fold the rectangle into half again so that your folded raw edges will touch each other. Press. You can also use an iron box to press the fabric. Pin the rectangle to keep the folds together.

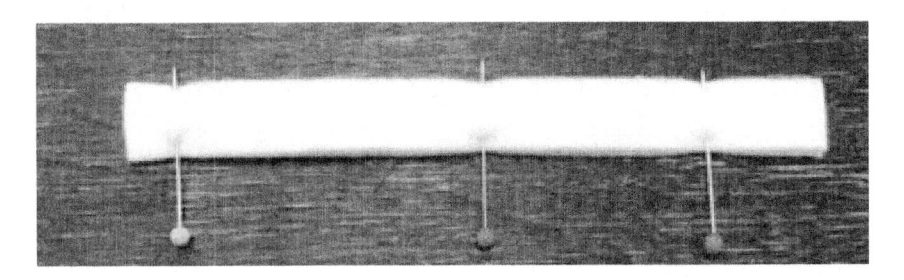

Step 12

Add stitches to the open edges of the rectangle strip and use 1/8 inch seam allowance. Now you have made the hanger for your stocking.

Now insert the hanger at the raw edges on the top opening of your stocking. Fold the hanger into U-shape and insert and insert the hanger between the stocking fabric and stitch it.

If you had already sewn the topstitch to the edges like in our case above, you can add finishing trims to the edges of the U-shaped hanger and then stitch it on the side of your stocking. You can add a decorative stitch on the outside to make it look even more beautiful.

With these simple steps, you can make your own Christmas stocking. Do more practice with different patterns for your family. If you want better results, you can pre-prep the fabrics by washing, drying, and pressing the seams. You can always customize the fabric based on your preferences and sew your Christmas stocking.

Chapter Summary

You can easily make your own Christmas stocking in simple steps. After learning these steps, you will never buy a Christmas stocking again. You can use an old stocking to measure the measurements of your new Christmas stocking or you can decide to make large size stockings.

There are different patterns you can choose to make your Christmas stockings. You can make different patterns for yourself or for your loved ones. Your family can choose a fabric of their choice for you to go ahead to make a Christmas stocking for them.

You can use the same fabric for both the outer layer and the lining or choose a different fabric.

Celebrate this Christmas with your own homemade Christmas stocking!

In the next chapter, you will learn how to make snack bags.

Chapter Nine: Snack Bags

Snack bags are a great accessory for your home. They are perfect for keeping your snacks fresh.

More people are now investing in eco-friendly and reusable snack bags to cut down on the use of plastic. Switching to the use of reusable snack bags will not only help in reducing environmental pollution but also prevent the plastics from ending up in oceans or landfills thus affecting wildlife.

Snack bags are often made of either silicon material or cloth. Some of these bags are microwave safe and you can dish-wash them, making them easy to clean and re-heat.

Image source: Alex Lab/ Shutterstock

Snack bags come in different sizes, making them great for every type of lunch or snack. The smaller size snack bags are ideal for dividing your snacks into smaller portions, for example, into portions that are 100 calories per serving. Extra smaller bags are great for storing your nuts so you can bring them with you.

These bags are also good for packaging pizza slices, sandwiches, cookies, chips, vegetables, fruits, etc. Just grab your favorite bag and go snacking!

Since you can bring them with you, you can create your own custom made plastic bags for food storage. Making your own snack bag is wallet-friendly, all you need is to invest in a durable material and make a variety of sizes at home.

If you have school-aged kids, you may find it more taxing to look for containers with matching tops each morning five days a week. A reusable snack and sandwich bag can come to your rescue.

How to make your own snack bag

It is super-fast to make your snack bag at home. You can also choose your favorite fabric and add decorative finishing to make it more attractive.

Materials needed

- Woven cotton fabric (12 inch * 7 inch)
- Ripstop nylon lining or laminated fabric(12 inch * 7 inch)
- All-purpose serger thread

- Scissors

- Rotary cutter or cutting mat

- Pins or clips

- Fray check

- Serger machine

Step 1

Align the woven fabric and the lining together with the right sides facing each other. Pin the fabrics together. Sew the short edges of the fabric together with ¼ inch seam allowance.

Step 2

Turn the right side out and press the seam although it is impossible for the Ripstop nylon to hold the press. It will make the seam look neat.

Step 3

Fold the edges on the left short end with the right sides together and clip.

Step 4

Fold the other short end with the right sides facing each other and line the ends of the short edges together.

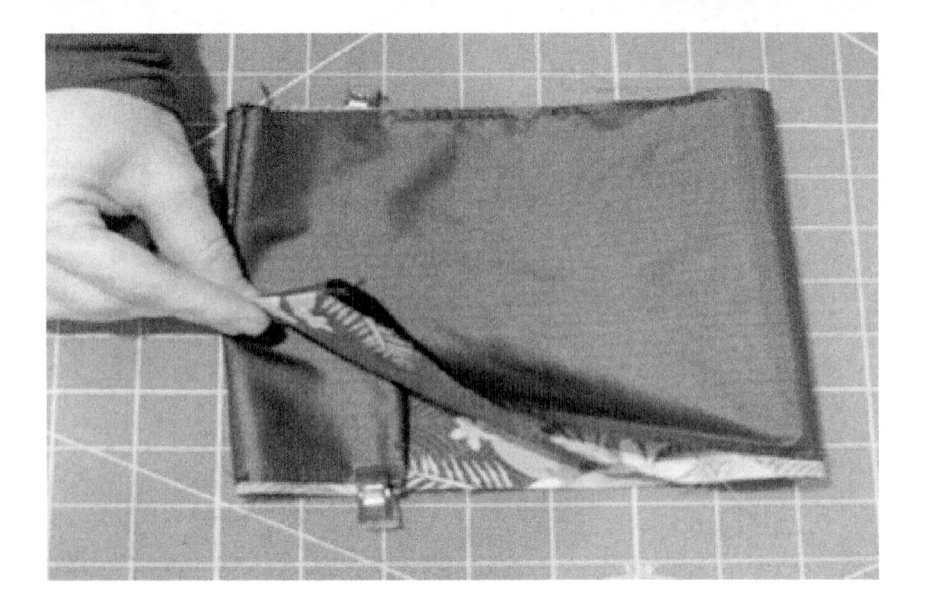

Clip the sides of the folded fabric.

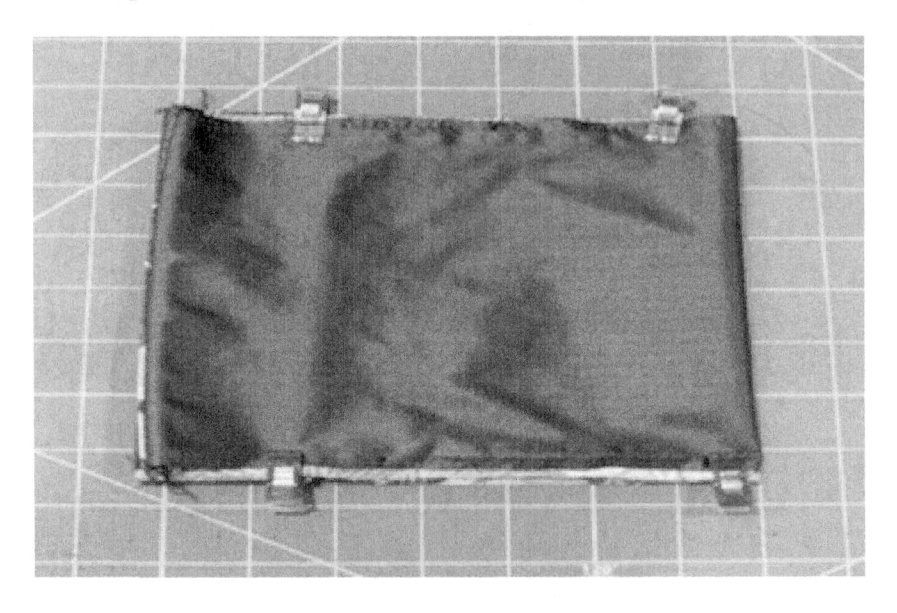

Step 5

Serge both sides with a seam allowance of ¼ inch using overlock stitch. Use a tapestry needle to tuck in the extra thread chain.

Alternatively, you can cut the excess thread chain and apply fray check on the thread chain to lock the stitches.

Step 6

You can decide to box the corners of your snack bag or just leave it as it is. If you don't want box corners for your snack bag, just turn it right side out and you're good to go.

Step 7

If you want to add box corners on the bag, turn the wrong side out and put your fingers inside the bag to flatten the bottom side, and press. You can also use a small awl to pull the corners. Avoid using any sharp object or scissors that can make a hole at the corners.

Clip around ½ inch and serger the bottom. At the same time, trim the excess fabric.

Draw a triangle around the corner edger and stitch the bag with an overlock stitch. Do the same to the other bottom end of the bag.

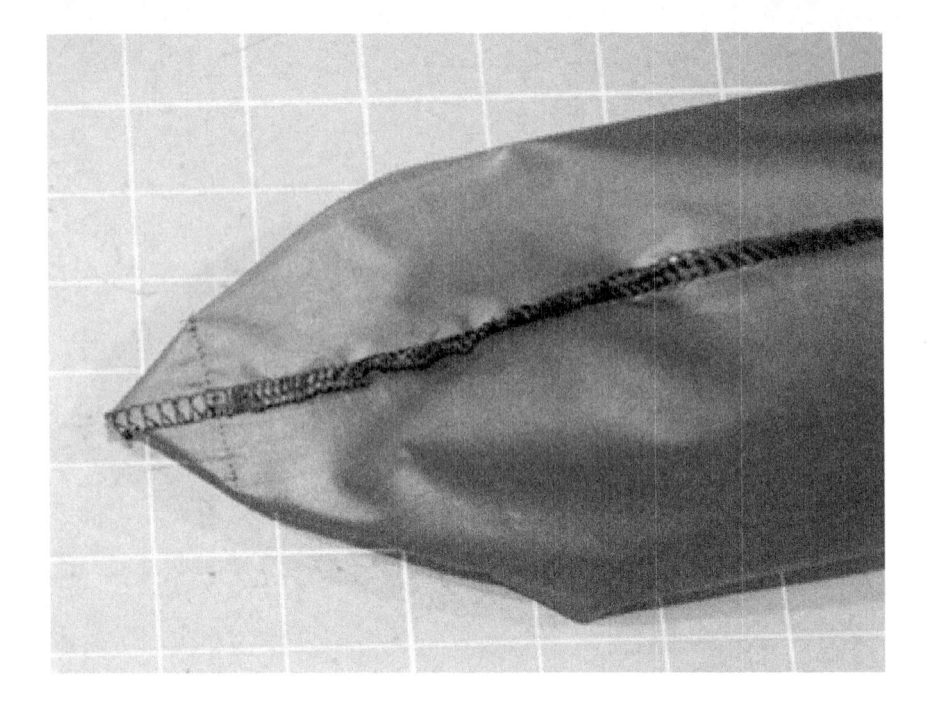

Step 8

Turn your snack bag with the right side out, use a blunt object or your fingers to push the triangle flap up the side of the seam. Tack in the triangle on the side of the snack bag by stitching a ditch from the outside of the bag. Do the same to create a box corner on the other side.

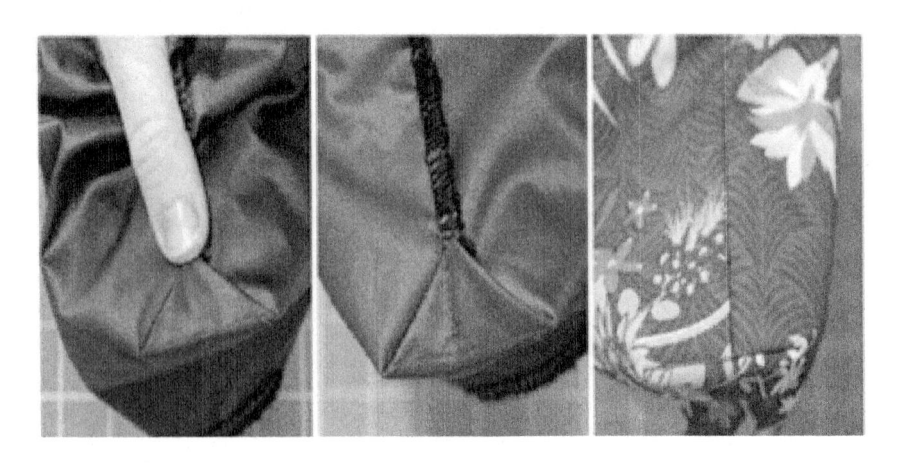

Step 9

Pack your snacks and turn the folded-down piece (folded pocket with the lining) over the open edge of the bag to enclose your snacks inside as shown on the left image.

Now your snack bag is ready to go! Pack your cookies or sandwich and bring them to the picnic or carry your lunch snacks.

Creating a snack bag with rectangle corners

It is advisable to wash and press your fabric before you begin any project, especially if you're working with cotton fabrics. You can start by washing both the cotton fabric and lining. Press the cotton fabric, do not press the nylon lining.

Step 1

Cut the cotton fabric and nylon lining of the same size (12 inches * 7 inches). You can even create a paper template to help you in measuring accurate fabric size. Place the fabric in a cutting mat and use an acrylic ruler to make your work easier with the rotary blade.

Step 2

Line the cut cotton fabric and a ripstop nylon lining together such that the right sides face each other. Make sure the edges match each other and pin around the bounders.

Step 3

Start sewing one of the long sides of the fabric with ¼ inch seam allowance and leave about a half gap at the beginning of your stitch. Remove the pins as you continue sewing to avoid damaging your machine or breaking needles when you sew over them.

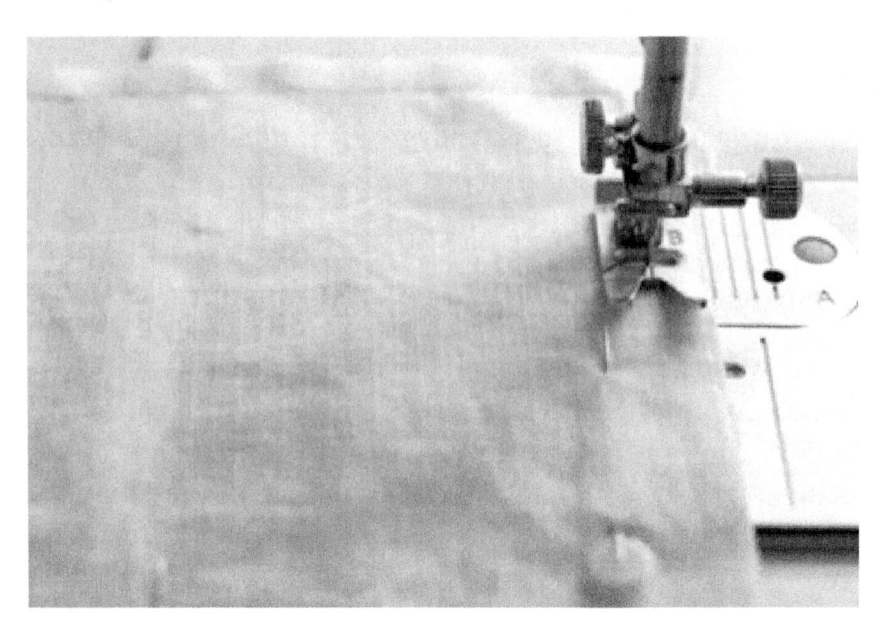

Sew all around all sides of the fabric leaving a gap of around 2 inches between the start and end of your stitch. The gap will enable you to turn the right side out.

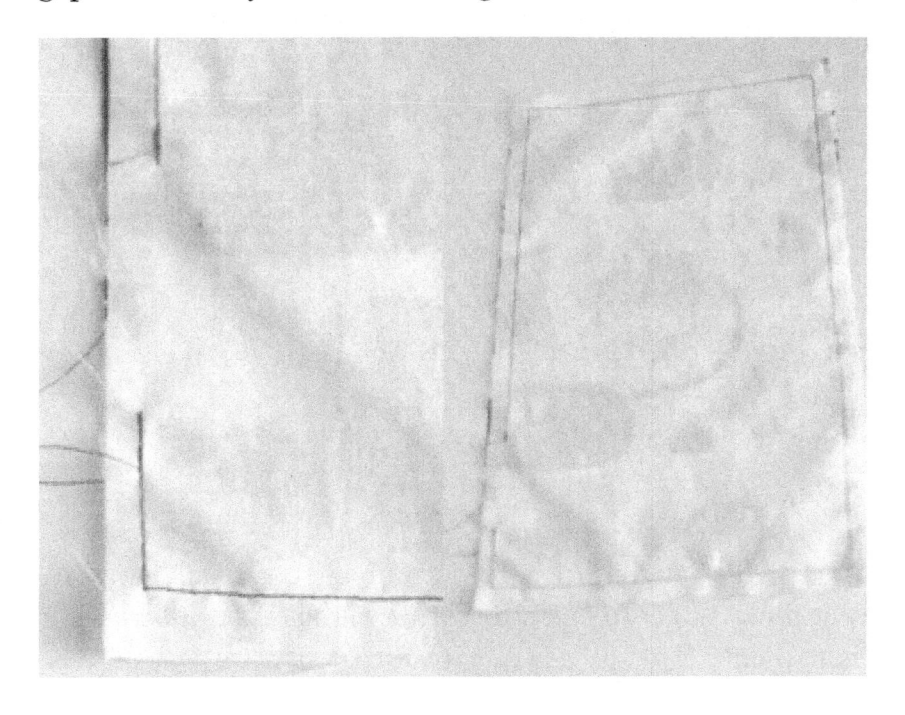

Step 4

Trim the corners and be careful not to cut the seams. This will ensure the corners of your bag are not bulky and look good when you turn right side out.

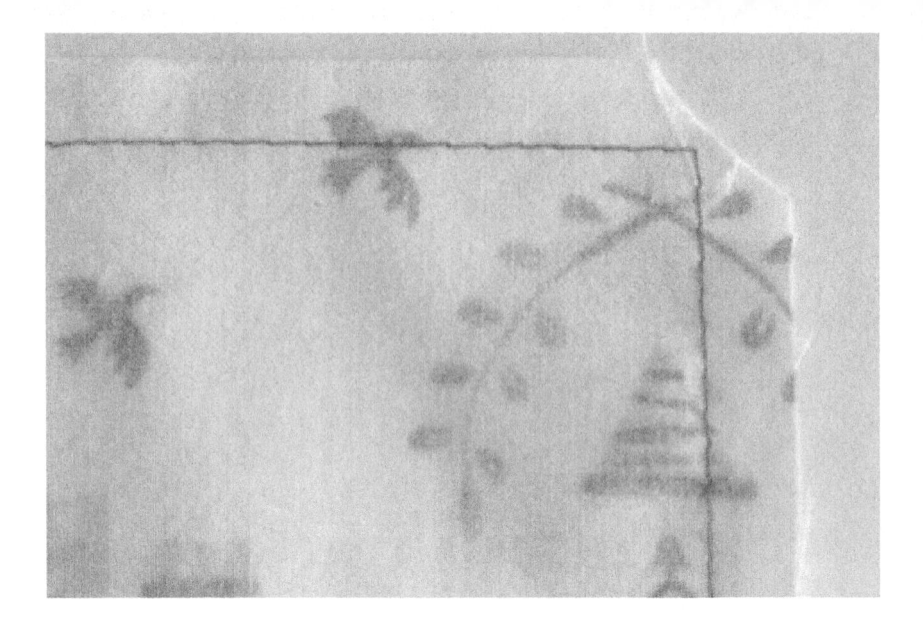

Step 5

Use the gap to turn right side out and use a small awl or your pinky finger to push the corner of the fabric and make them pointy.

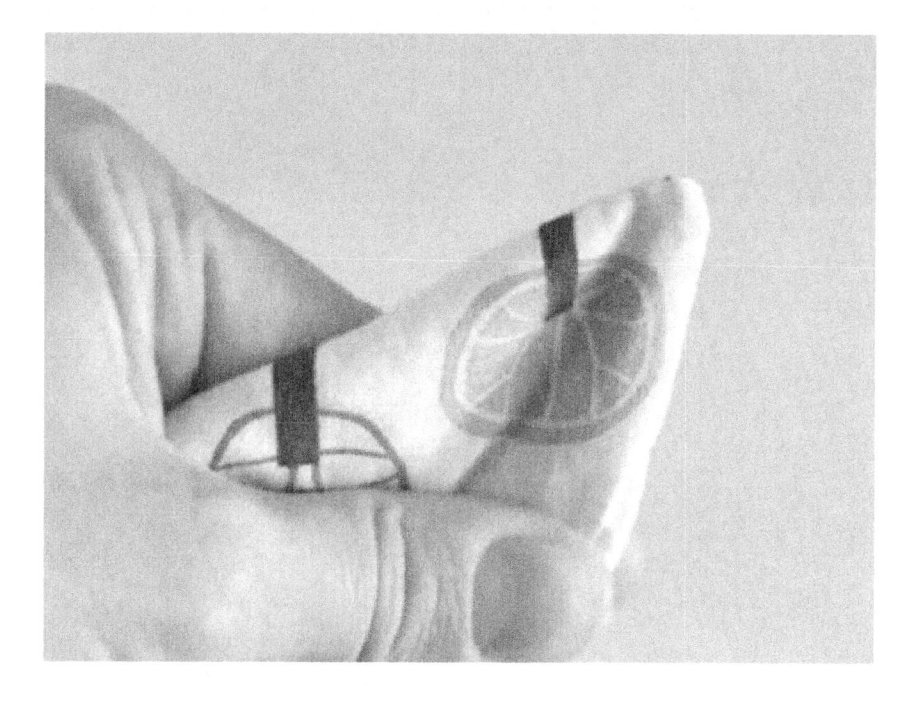

Step 6

Press the corners of the two pieces, or iron around the corners to remove any wrinkles. Only iron the cotton fabric and not the ripstop nylon lining. Ironing the seams will make the fabric look nice and flat.

The seam allowance around the gap should be folded in.

Step 7

Turn the fabric with the wrong side out (ripstop nylon side up) and place it on a flat surface. Fold the left short end towards the other short end, but leave 2 inches at the top.

Step 8

Fold the remaining 2 inches down to create a flap. This will leave you with the envelope-like shape of your rectangle. Put a pin around the flap and then sew the sides.

Step 9

Serge along the edges of the short ends of the fabric. Make sure your needle stitches around the corners and edges of the fabric. You can reverse the stitch at the start to secure your stitches. Stitch all the way down until the flap and entire short end is sewn.

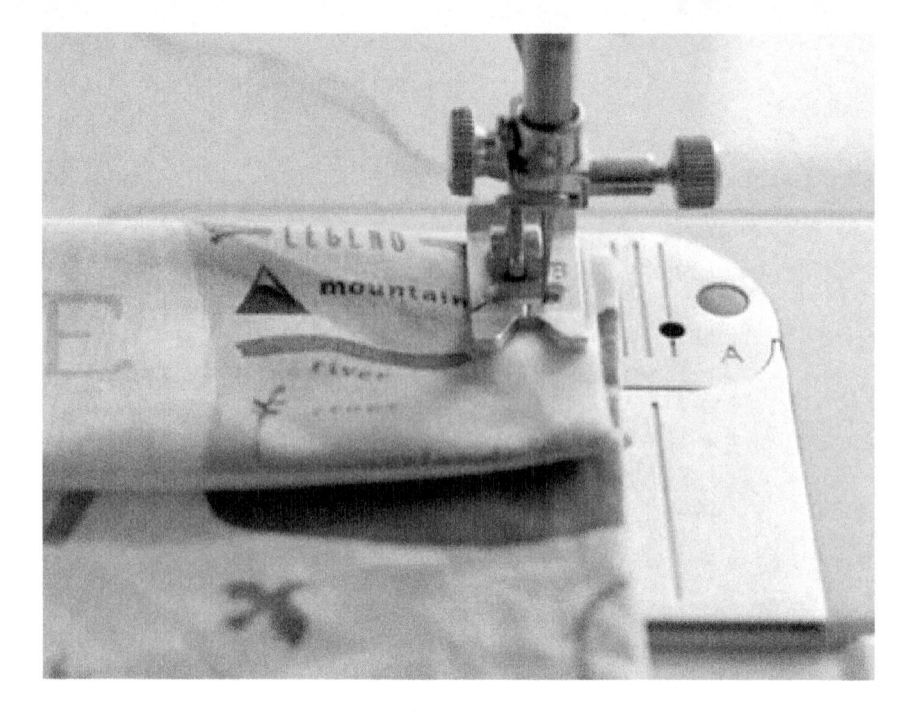

Repeat the same process on the other side of the short end.

Now your snack bag is ready for use. Just push up the flap and push the corners with your hands. Put your favorite snacks inside and you're good to go!

Once you add your food inside the bag, you can fold the long edge into the bag. Do not overpack your food in the bag, otherwise some of it will fall out. Instead, make a bigger size snack bag to accommodate more snacks.

You can also add a decorative stitch at the folded-down pocket of the bag to make it more beautiful. If you're making the snack bag for your kids, a decorative stitch using elastic thread or a beaded cord will contribute to the beauty of the snack bag.

If you have any scrap fabrics, you will never throw them away again. With these simple steps, you can create a snack bag for your family use. You can make various sizes of snack bags and use them to store your foodstuffs and snacks.

The snack bags are budget-friendly and easy to clean. You only need to turn them inside out and wash them. If you're stuffing in dry foodstuff, you can pack up the bag several times before you can wash it with your regular laundry.

Chapter Summary

Snack bags are very essential in a modern home: you can use them to store foodstuffs around your home, or pack cookies and sandwiches for your children when going to school. These bags have multiple uses and they are easy to make.

It won't take you more than ten minutes to make a snack bag. You can make different sizes for your family based on the width of the fabric. They don't have to be only one size if you're making them for your family.

You can include different designs and let your kids choose the fabric and design they love.

These reusable snack bags are easy to make and you can wash them with your regular laundry. Grab any scrap fabric and make your own reusable snack bag!

In the next chapter, you will learn how to make a holiday tree napkin.

Chapter Ten: Holiday Tree Napkin

It is almost December and friends and family will start to flock to your home. You'll want to start shopping for the perfect gift for your friends and loved ones. Or you're planning to cook delicious meals and set up a perfect Christmas table for your family.

Regarding setting up your table, there is so much you can do! Converting your napkins to an adorable tree will make a perfect addition to your dining table. No matter the design scheme you're using, your table will look lively.

Image source: Mama_Mia/Shutterstock

To add a personal touch to the designs, you can make your own tree napkins for your table. Learning how to make the Christmas tree napkin will up your holiday table setting game.

Making napkins for your holiday tree

You can make your own classy modern napkins and transform them into a Christmas tree in simple steps. Creating your own custom made napkins for setting up the Christmas tree not only impress your guests but also leaves your dining setting looking more elegant.

How to create napkins

You can make your napkins in two ways:

1. Reversible napkins: These are easy to make napkins and suitable for beginners. They are two-sided and reversible making them great for adding some color to your table.

2. Mitered corners: This type of napkins has hemmed edges and usually made of linen material and they're unlined. These are the most common traditional napkins in every household.

Although this tutorial is going to concentrate on how to make mitered corner napkins and fold them to form a Christmas tree, I will briefly show you how to make reversible napkins.

Reversible napkins

The best fabrics to use in making napkins are pure cotton and linen since they can absorb any mess and they're easy to fold.

To make your napkin, you need:

- Fine linen
- Quilting cotton (good if you want to make napkins with patterns)
- Drill
- Cotton duck

Cut and iron the fabric

Cut two pieces of fabric based on your size and add 6 mm seam allowance. In our case, let's cut two equal pieces that measure 16 inches * 16 inches with ¼ inch seam allowance. Iron the fabric to remove any creases.

Step 1

Match the two cut pieces together with the right sides together and pin all around the fabric.

Step 2

Stitch all around the fabric with ¼ inch seam allowance and leave a gap of 2inch on one side to allow you to turn the napkin right side out.

Step 3

Clip the corners of the fabric to avoid any bulkiness around the corners of the napkin.

Step 4

Turn the right side out via the gap. Use the awl or back of your pencil to poke out the corners and press the seams. Press inside the seam allowance at the gap and add a top stitch all around the napkin. Ensure your stitch is around 1/8 inch from the edges of the napkin. This will close the gap as well.

Step 5

Give your napkin a final press using the iron to make the napkin look neat and flat. Your napkin is ready for setting your dinner table.

Making mitered napkins

Mitered napkins are great if you want to decorate them later like making a Christmas tree. To make your napkin, you can use linen material or any other material that is highly absorbent and is made of natural fibers such as cotton.

Step 1

Cut the fabric into a square that measures 16 inches * 16 inches. If you have a plain fabric with no wrong or right side, it will be great for making the napkin holiday tree.

Step 2

On the wrong side, fold the edges with ¼ inch and another ½ inch on one end of the fabric and press the folds.

Step 3

On the next edge, fold the edges by the same amounts of ¼ inch followed by ½ inch. Press the folds. Thick will create a thick fabric at the corners making it look bulk when you stitch the napkin that's why you have to clip the corners to remove the bulkiness.

Step 4

Open the folds, you will notice that the presses have created some creases on the fabric. You can make the creases with your tailor's chalk or drawing pencil to make it easy to know where to clip.

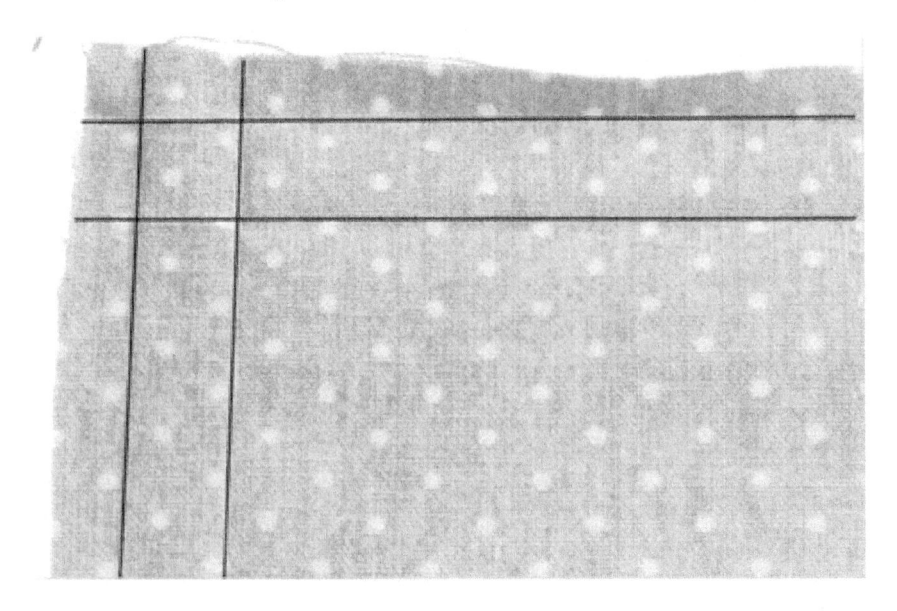

Step 5

Mark a diagonal line touching the corners of the center square.

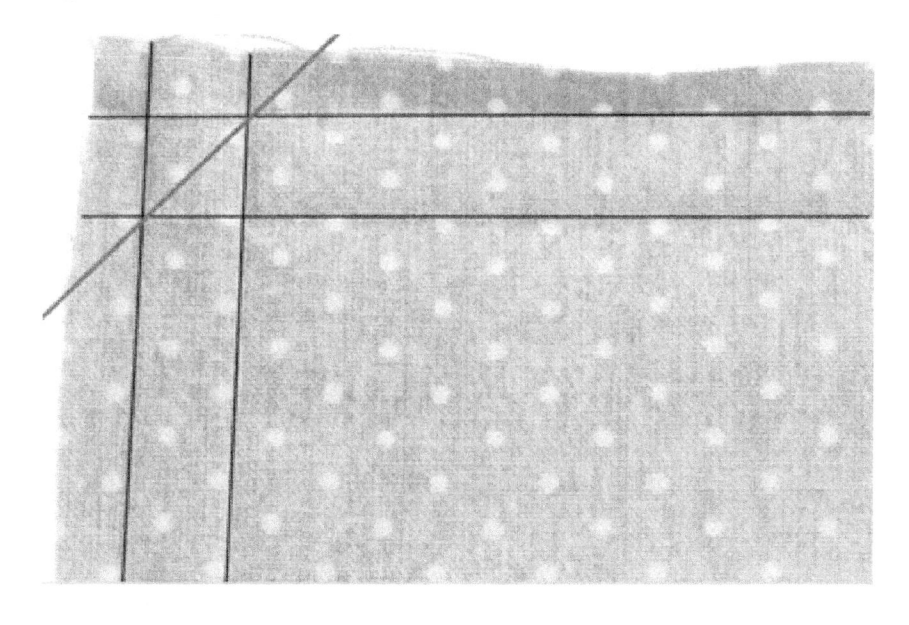

Step 6

Cut the fabric across the marked area.

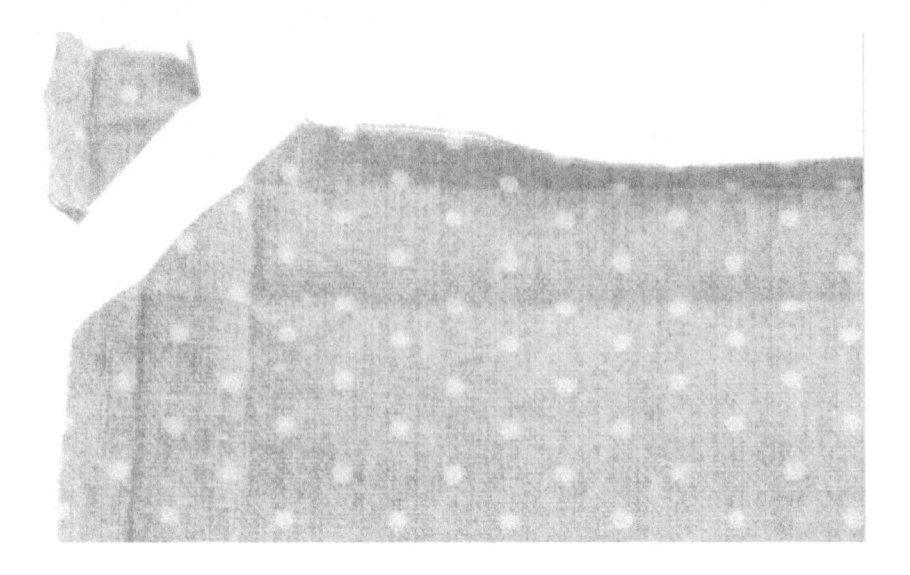

Step 7

Mark another diagonal line on the inner crease fold as shown below.

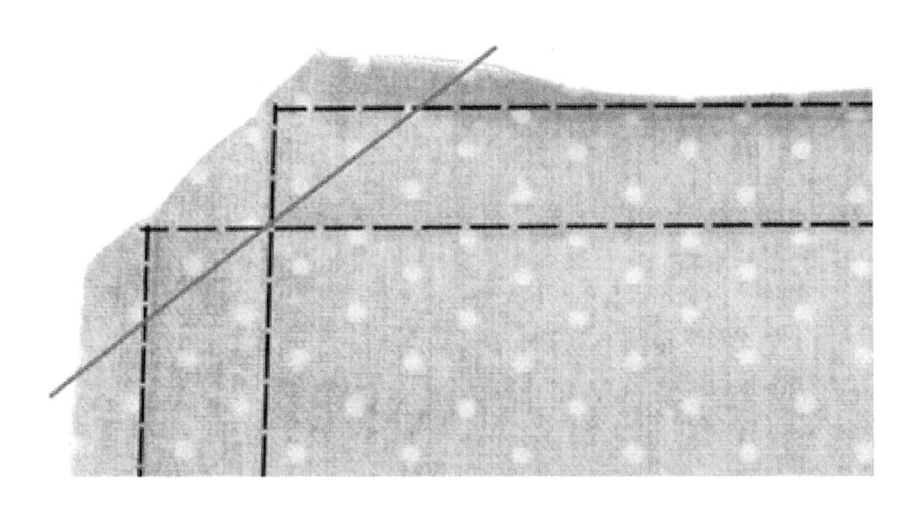

Step 8

Fold along the mark and press it.

Step 9

Now fold again the pressed edge and pin the corner. Repeat the same steps for the remaining corners.

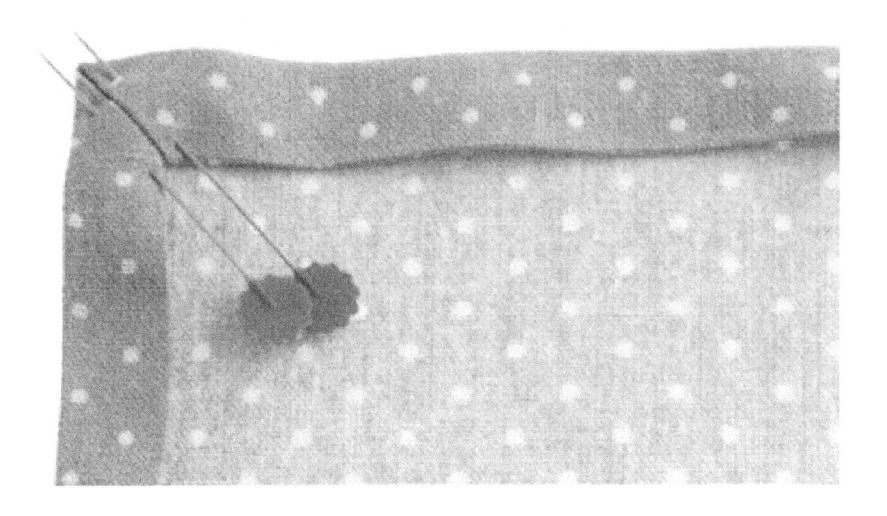

Step 10

Stitch hem edges all around the napkin.

Now your napkin is ready for use.

Folding a napkin tree

If you already have the napkins, you can go ahead and fold them into a Christmas tree.

Materials required

- Cotton napkin (16 inches * 16 inches)
- Tiny bow
- Pin

Steps to fold the napkins into tiers

Folding the napkins to look like a Christmas tree is a great addition to your table décor this festive season. You can make a good tree napkin using fabric made of 100% natural fibers such as cotton and linen. You can also use fabrics made from a blend of cotton/polyester.

Step 1

Iron the napkin to have a crisper looking tree napkin, although ironing is optional. Place the square napkin on a flat surface. It doesn't matter which side is facing up. If the napkin already has a tag, remove it because you don't want it to show on your final design.

Step 2

Pick your square napkin and fold it in half to form a rectangle shape.

Step 3

Fold it again to get a smaller square. All the corners of the napkin should line up with each other.

Step 4

Rotate the folded napkin so that it creates a diamond shape. The loose corners should be at the bottom as shown above.

Step 5

Pick the first bottom layer and fold it towards the top point.

Step 6

Continue to fold the corners up with each corner layer staggering slightly below each other. Fold each layer of the napkin to the top leaving an inch between the folds. Press the folds in place.

Step 7

Flip the napkin over while holding the folds. You can easily flip the napkin by placing one hand at the bottom while the other is holding the folds at the top then carefully flip the napkin. Press each layer as you fold.

Step 8

Now fold both sides of the napkin together. Fold the lower outside to the opposite side and align each of the panels at the top to form a triangle shape.

Step 9

Repeat the same process to the other corner. This will create a sharp pointed edge at the bottom of the fabric.

Step 10

Hold the top folded layers so that they don't unfold then flip the napkin over to the front side. Rotate the napkin to have a cute Christmas tree napkin fold. You can stop here or continue adding more decorations to your Christmas tree.

Step 11

Fold the top layer of the napkin to the top to create the peak of your Christmas tree. You can also fold the top layer underneath itself to form a neat triangle shape.

Step 12

Tuck the second layer underneath the upper layer to a triangle-like shape. Press the fold.

Step 13

Tuck the other layers underneath each of the upper layers and create a beautiful Christmas tree.

Step 14

You can add a tiny bow at the peak to add more finishing to your Christmas tree. Pin it at the peak.

Step 15

Place the folded napkin on an empty plate and make sure the folds are still in place. Now your Christmas tree folded napkin is ready.

To prevent the folds from coming undone, you can use pins to pin them in place. You can also add some decorations to the folded napkins. For example, you can tie a skinny ribbon to form little bows, use cinnamon sticks at the bottom to make the napkin resemble a real tree, or use paper cut-out stars and other ornaments.

You can also make your folded napkin sit on the plate instead as shown below. All you need is to open the bottom of the napkin.

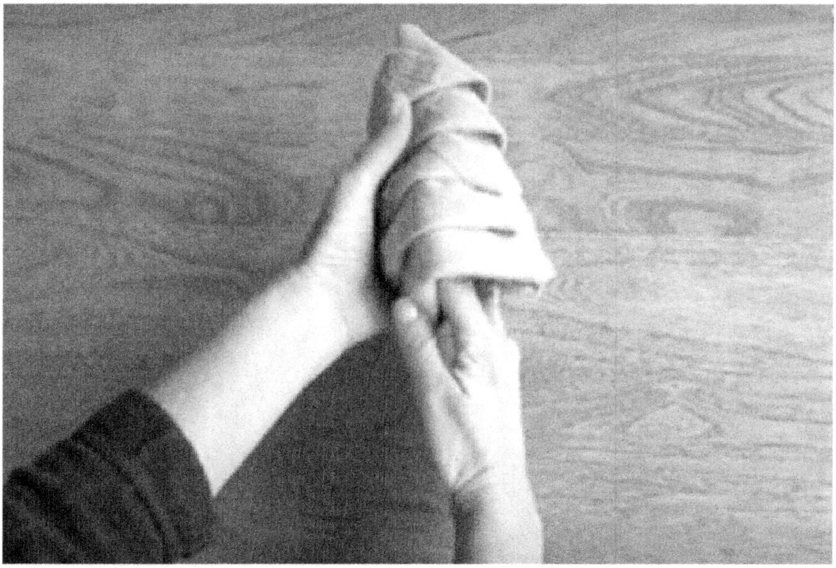

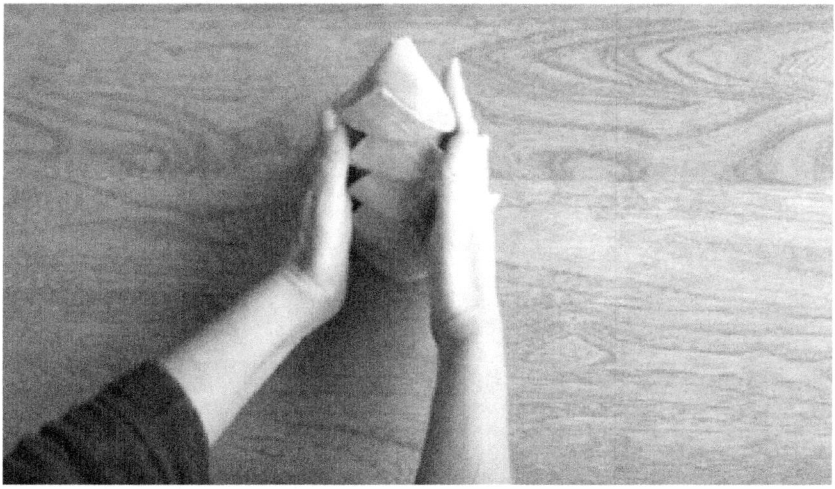

Chapter Summary

Creating your own DIY napkin gives you a personalized look at your dining setting. You can use any absorbent fabric like cotton or linen or a blend of the two. The cotton fabric or linen makes it easy to add folds to the napkin especially when making a napkin Christmas tree.

There are two methods you can use to make your napkins: reversible napkins and mitered corner napkins. Mitered corner napkins using plain material are great for making a Christmas tree.

Choose a napkin with the color of your choice then proceed to make the napkin tree. Follow the above step by step guide to making a neat and beautiful Christmas tree. You can add some decorations to your tree or just leave it like that and place it on a plate.

You can go ahead and decorate your dining table with these Christmas tree napkins.

In the next chapter, you will learn how to make your own facemask.

Chapter Eleven:
How To Make Face Mask

In these times when face masks are a necessity, you can easily make one at home using your serger machine.

Since you need a face mask every day when going out, you can make several for your family to protect them. Homemade face masks can add a degree of protection although they may not be as effective as medical grade masks.

Homemade masks are great for running errands and provides you with a visual cue that you have to maintain social distancing protocols. They also ensure you don't touch your face, nose, and mouth during this COVID 19 pandemic.

Image source: Victoria Chudinova/Shutterstock

Today, face masks are becoming part of our fashion as a response to providing protection; more reason why you should custom fit them. There are different designs you can use to make your face mask. In this tutorial, I will show you how to make face masks in two ways.

Making an easy design face mask

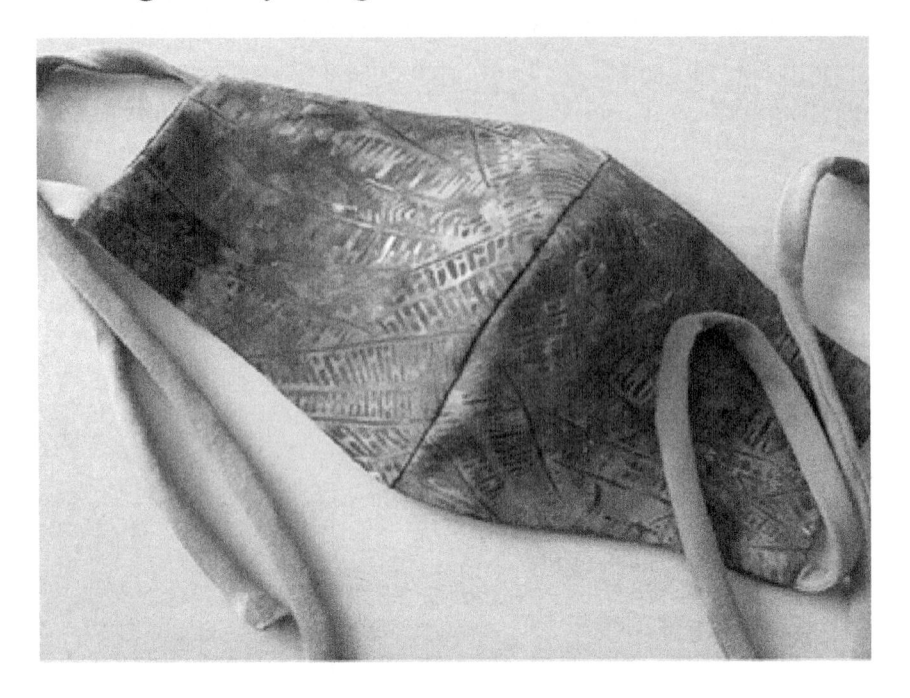

This is one of the most common self-made designs. It is great for those who wear glasses since it has a more comfortable shape. You can easily make this design with your overlock stitch or even the regular sewing machine.

With this design, you can add an additional layer of filter fabric to maximize your protection. Any 4-thread overlock machine can do a marvelous job in sewing this mask. The MTC (micro thread control) feature in your machine will give you excellent results when sewing the rounded seam.

Material required

- 2 pieces of the outer fabric
- 2 pieces of the middle lining (mouth lining)
- 2 pieces of side-lining (cheeks)

- 4 pieces of cut straps (knit cross-cut)

Machine settings

To start sewing, you have to adjust your tension to default settings or increase the upper looper tension and reduce the lower looper tension. Use a scrap material to test your stitch formation. If your needle thread is loose, then adjust the needle thread tension to default.

Alternatively, you can increase the tension of the left needle thread and reduce tension on the lower looper. If the right needle is loose, you can adjust the tension settings to default. Otherwise, increase the right needle thread tension.

Based on your fabric and thread, you can adjust the stitch length from 0.8 to 4. Adjust your differential feed from 0.7 to 2. If you need flat seams, set your differential feed to be between 1 and 2. To accommodate the fabric stretch, adjust the differential feed to between 0.7-1.

You also need to adjust the seam width based on your needs.

When using the right needle, the stitch formation should be set to a minimum of 3mm seam as shown in the first stitch. The last stitch formation shows a stitch using the left needle with the seam length set to 9mm.

If you have a balanced stitch, you can go ahead and start sewing.

Step 1

You can use a free downloaded Olson Mask pattern by Clayton Skousen & Rose Hedges to guide you in cutting the pieces of the fabric.

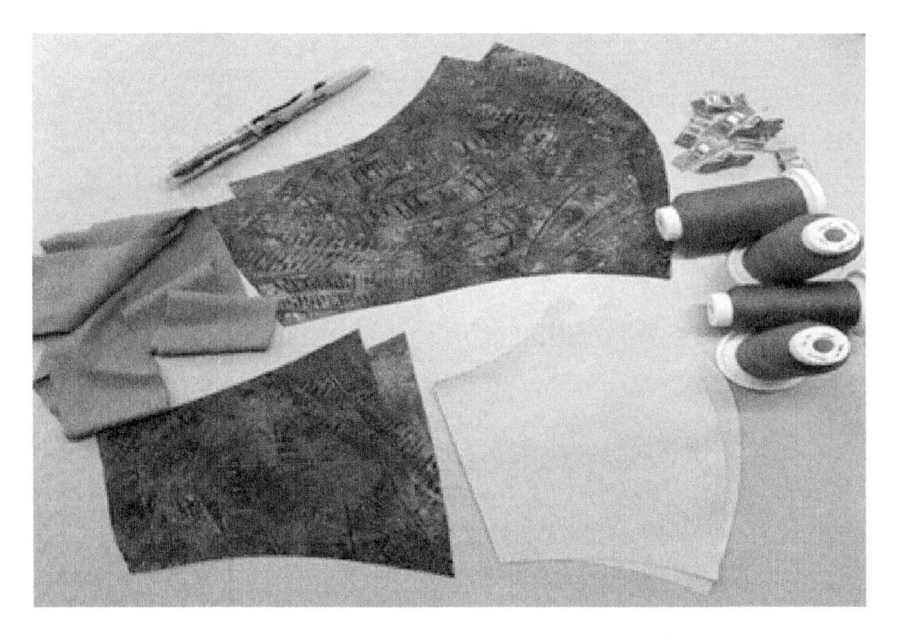

Step 2

Place the rounded outer fabric and the middle lining together with the right side facing each other. Pin them together.

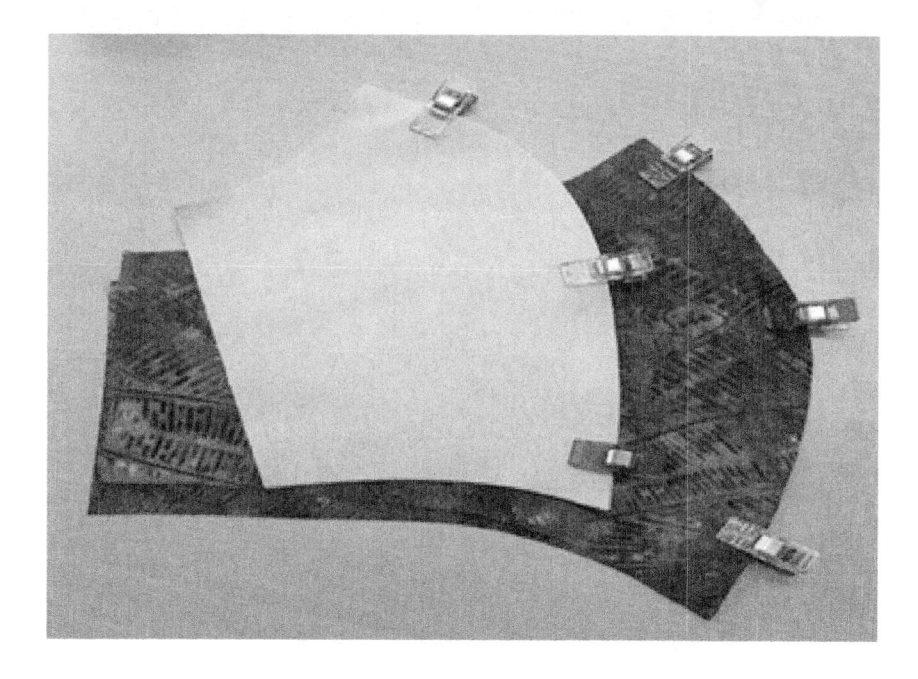

To get better results for the curved seam, pick a scrap fabric, and test the stitch. Set the MTC to +plus because you need loose loops for the curve so that the seam allowance remains flat and no bulkiness on the seam of the curve. You can adjust the MTC while sewing to get the right balance.

Step 3

Once you're satisfied with the results sew the seam on the middle lining and outer fabric curves.

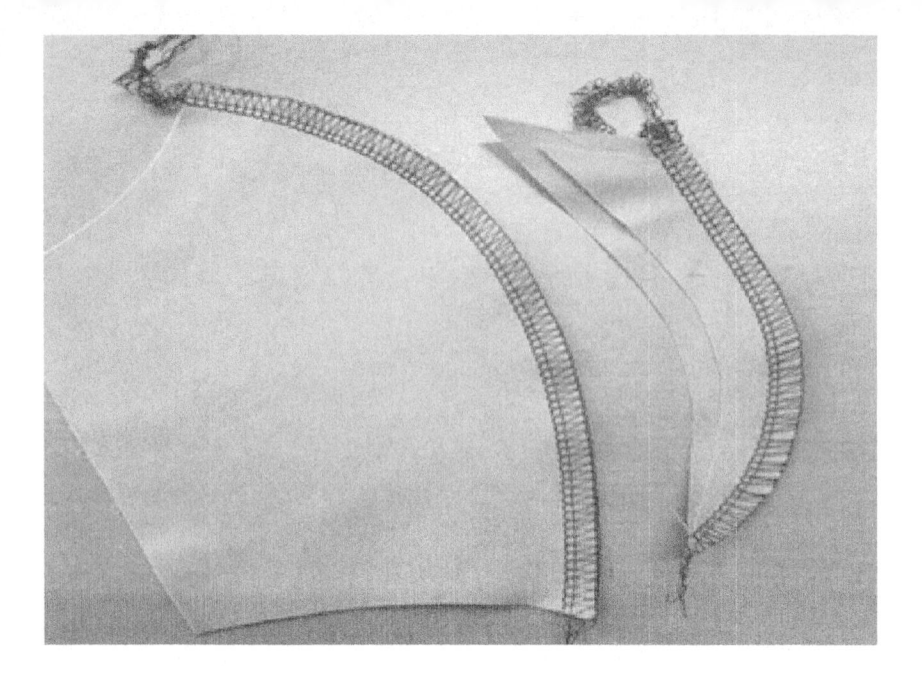

Step 4

Reset the MTC back to the default settings and stitch the next seam.

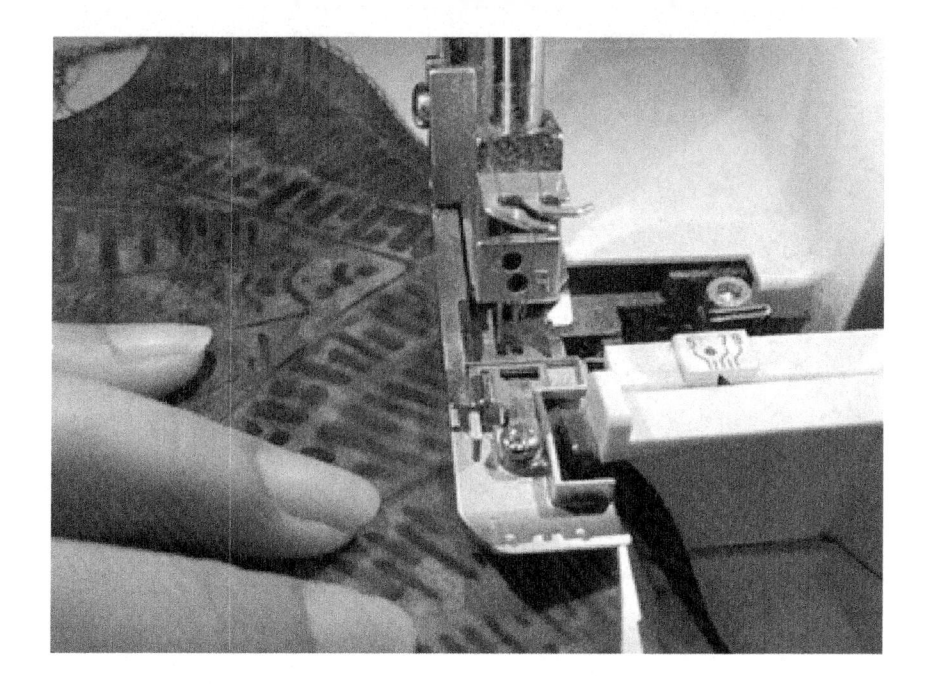

Step 5

Iron the seam allowance so that it lies flat on one side in the outer fabric and on the other side of the middle lining. This will prevent the formation of thick spots under your chin and on your nose that causes discomfort.

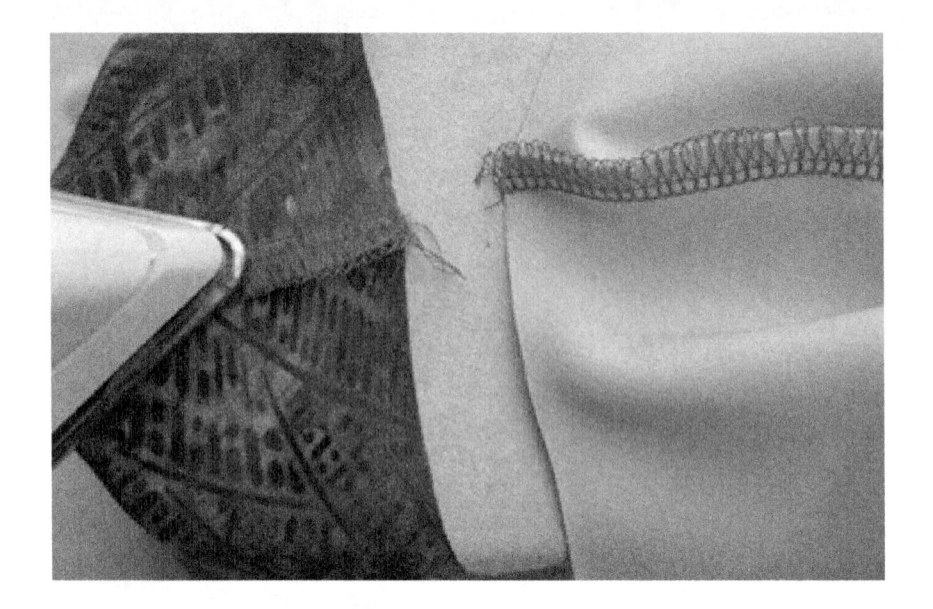

Step 5

Neaten the straight edges of your middle lining and those of the side-lining to securely hold them in place. Neatening stitches prevent fraying of raw edges as well as hold hems securely.

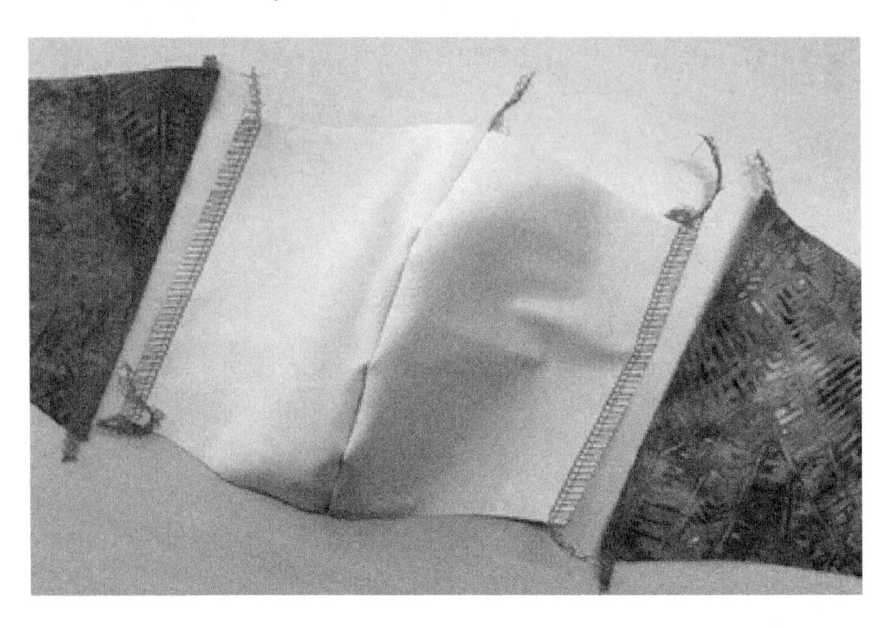

Step 6

Align the top edge of the outer fabric and the middle lining with the right side facing each other. Ensure the curved seam match and the seam allowance face away from each other. Pin the fabrics together.

Align the parts of the side lining and ensure the center lining is overlapping and pin them together.

Step 7

Place the mask sideways with the outer fabric on the outside. Cut the seam allowance of the middle lining to 3mm to prevent it showing after sewing the mask.

Pin the bottom edge of the mask. Use pins with a clear head so that you can easily remove them as you stitch.

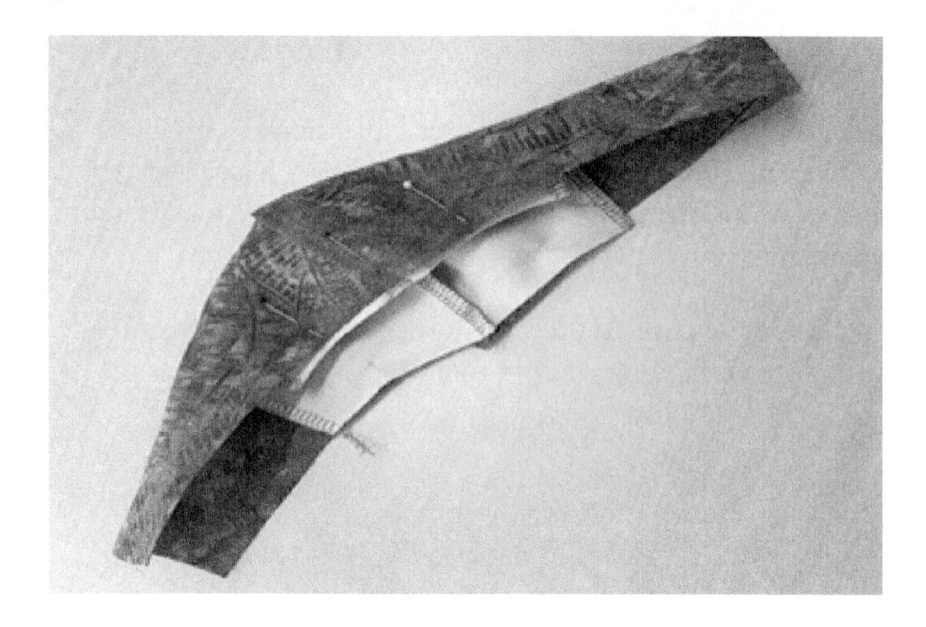

Step 8

Start stitching the mask. Adjust the stitch length to 2 or 2.5 and blade cutting width to be 6mm. Adjust your speed to be slow so that you can get a nice rounded shape. Do not stitch over the pins so you should remove them as you stitch.

To ensure your fabric doesn't slide, you can remove the pin in front of the presser foot.

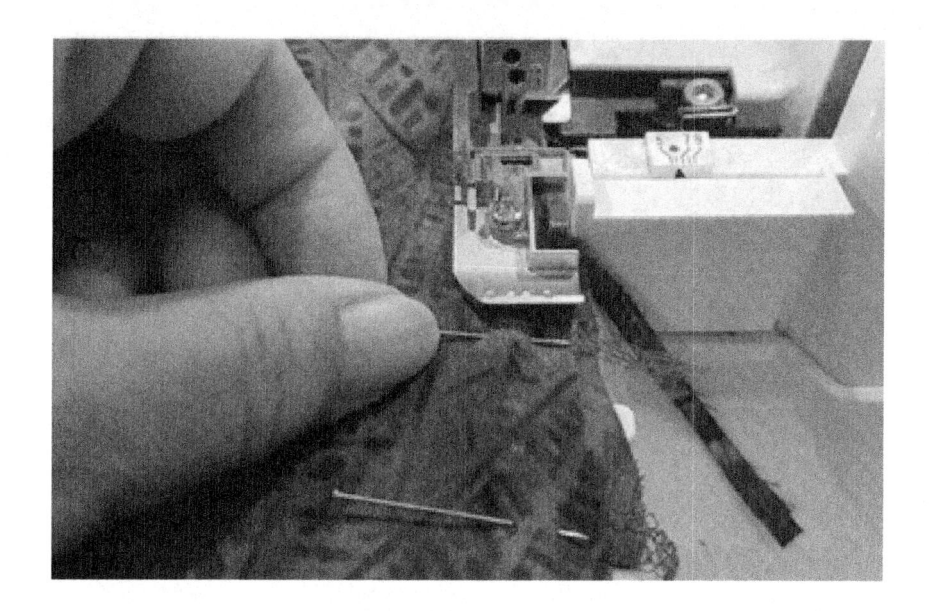

Step 9

When you get to the curved seam, ensure the seam allowance face away from each other to avoid bulkiness. It ensures you don't have unnecessary thick material around your nose or chin.

Step 10

After stitching both sides of the long edges, you can try the mask. If you want your ears to remain free, you can cut off 2cm from the sides of the fabric. You can adjust this after you have tried the mask on your face.

Step 11

Stitch the straps for your mask. You can stitch a tunnel strap using a 2cm seam allowance.

The stretch of your knit straps depends on the type of fabric you use. Always look for fabric that will be comfortable to wear. In this face mask, we will use knit fabric remnants to make the straps.

Sew an easy turning tube with your overlock machine. Set your stitch length to two so that the stitch can stretch to fit the fabric. If you're sewing a highly stretchy knit cross-cut fabric, then reduce the stitch length to 1.5 to increase the elasticity.

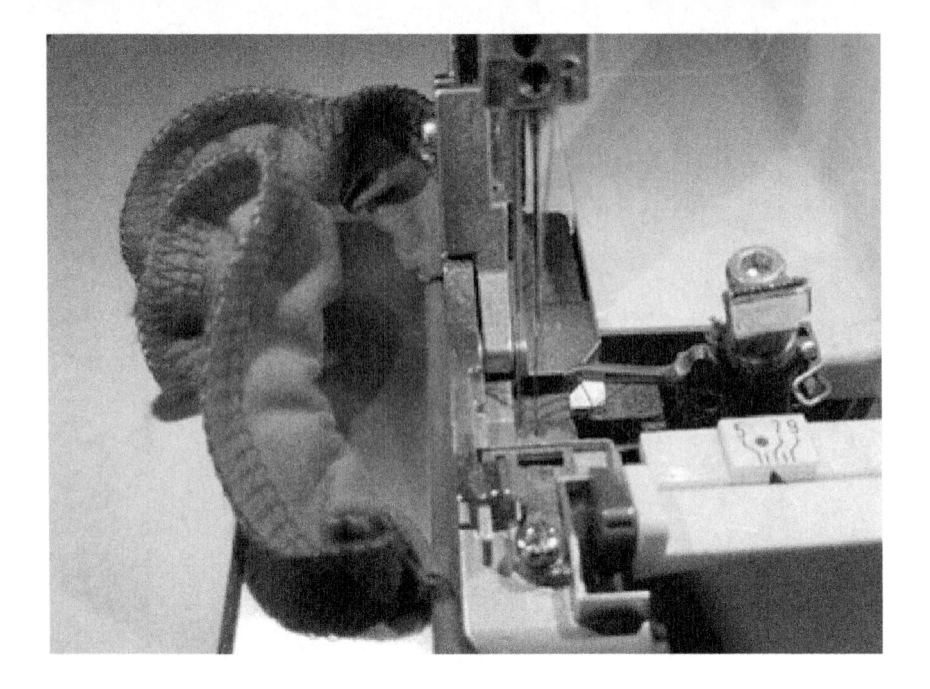

Step 12

Turn the tube to the right side out and proceed to insert the straps into your mask. Insert the straps from the middle to the side seams on both the top and bottom edges of the mask and pin the straps. Do the same on the other side of the mask and pin them.

Step 13

Stitch the side seam and remove the pin at the front of the presser foot.

Step 14

Secure the seam at the beginning and at the end by tying a knot on the thread chain and cut the excess chain. You can also use an inserter to insert the thread chain inside the seam.

Iron the seams to get better results and stability. Press seam allowance around the corners such that they are away from each other. You can easily turn the corners by inserting your finger around the corner to form a pyramid and then turn the corners.

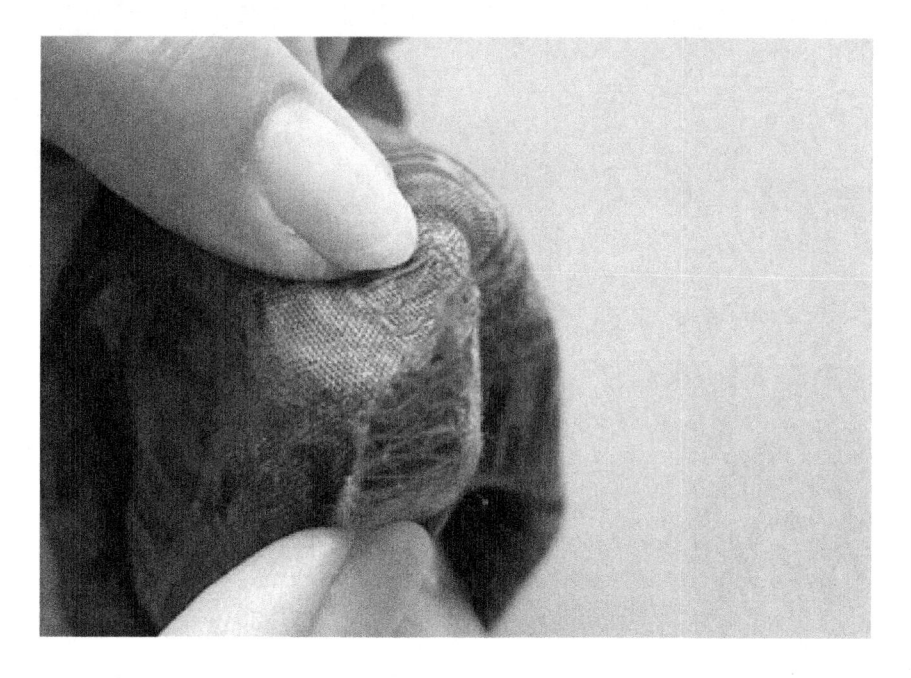

The straps can also help in shaping the corners of the mask

Step 15

Now turn the right side out and iron your mask to ensure the seams at the middle lining are flat and all the other seams from the four sides including the middle lining remain hidden.

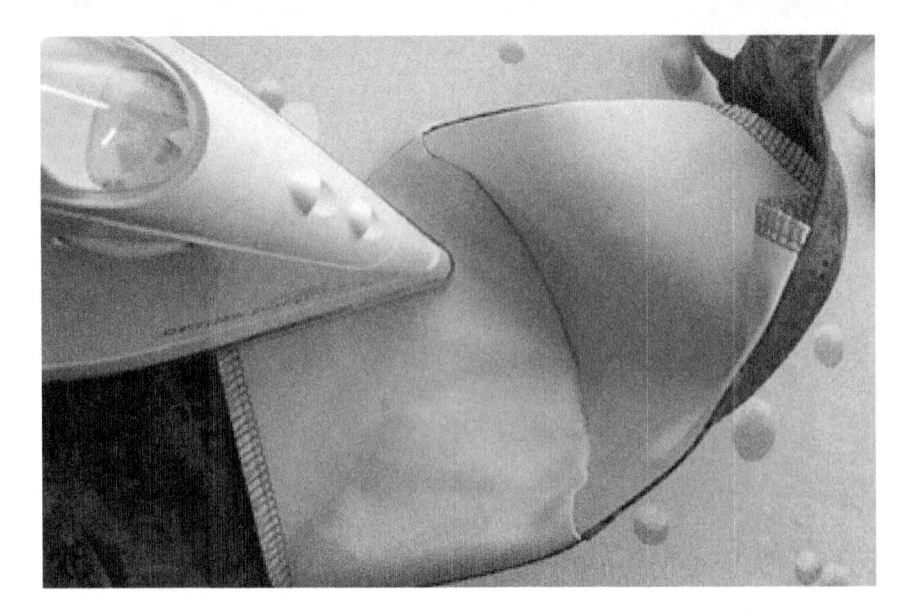

Step 16

You can also secure the end of the strap by pushing the edges back to the tunnel by 1 cm. you can use any tool that has a rounded tip to insert the edges. Iron the straps.

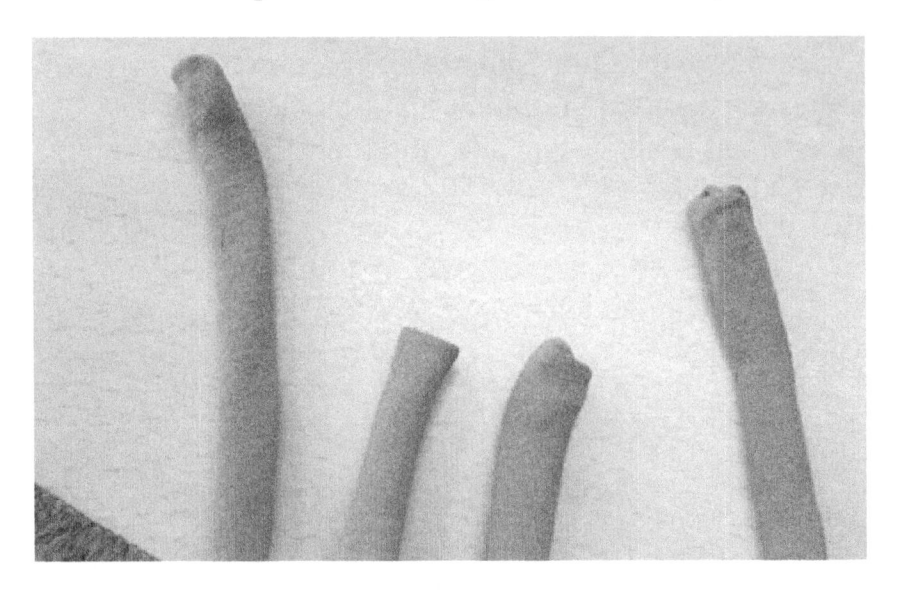

Step 17

Now your mask is ready for use. The mask has finished edges that make it look more professional.

Face Mask Design 2

If you want to make a more easy face mask, you can follow these few steps to make one for your family and friends.

Required materials

- 100 percent quilting cotton
- Cotton flannel
- Strip ¼ inch wide or Stretchy knit fabric 1 inch
- Twisty tie, pipe cleaner, or ribbon piece (optional)
- Filters (optional)
- Safety pin
- Serger Machine

Step 1

Wash and dry the fabrics. Cut two square pieces of fabric measuring 10.5 inches * 7 inches for adults and 9 inches * 7 inches for kids.

Step 2

Match the two pieces of fabric with the right sides facing each other and ensure the edges are aligned to each other and pin the pieces together.

Step 3

Shape the nose piece by using a twisty tie. You can also use a pipe cleaner or a wired ribbon to shape the nose piece. Place the wire or the twisty pie in the top center of the fabric. You can use either of the sides.

Step 4

Stitch the two pieces together at the top and bottom sides. You can use a cording foot that ensures the wire doesn't get caught up under the needles. If you don't have a cording foot, line up the pipe cleaner such that it runs between the two needles.

Slow down your serging speed as you stitch around the wire. If you don't have a serger machine, you can use a zigzag stitch to sew both the top and bottom edges of the fabric.

Step 5

Turn the fabric to have the right side out and press the seam to have a neat rectangle shape. Use your iron to make the seams sit as flat as possible.

Step 6

Turn your mask so it's upside down with the front fabric facing up. Start forming the pleats of the fabric. The newsprint checked the red & black fabric and the patterned fabric on the ruler mat.

Step 7

Use a light mist on the fabric to make it easy to create crisp pleats as you iron the fabric. Pinch a small piece of fabric on the side edges with your finger to form the first pleat. Make sure the pleat is pointing away from you. When you turn the mask, the outside pleat will face down.

The mask is upside down so add pleats facing away from you starting from the top edge. After forming your first pleat, press it hard and hand folds it on the ruler mat.

Step 8

Do the same process for the remaining pleats. You can form at least 2 more pleats of 3 inches on each side. Form masks on the newsprint fabric on the ruler mat.

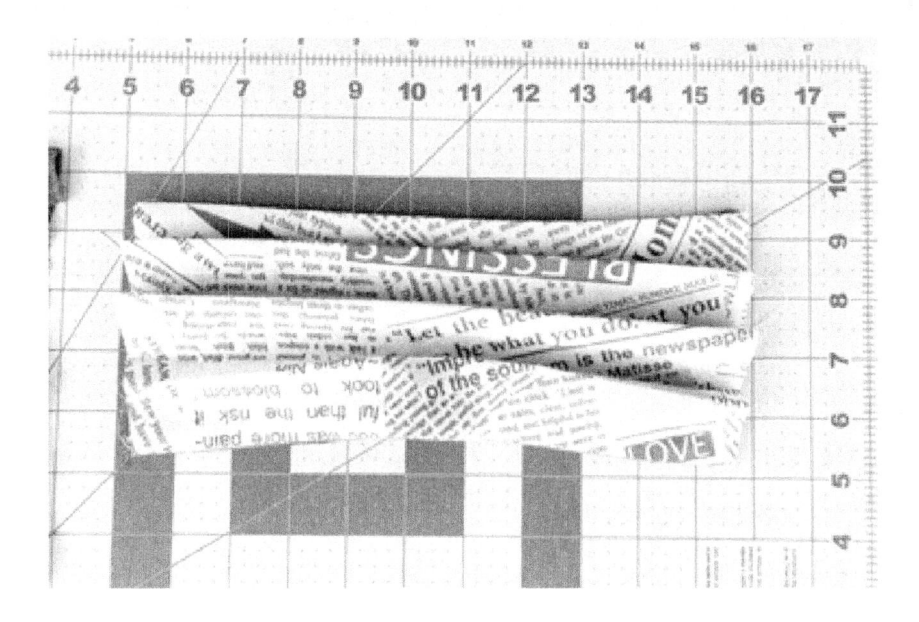

Step 9

Press the pleats and use a little steam to help in pressing the pleats. Therefore, it is not necessary to pin the pleats before you can stitch them. Hold the pleats with your hands as you serge along the edges of the mask.

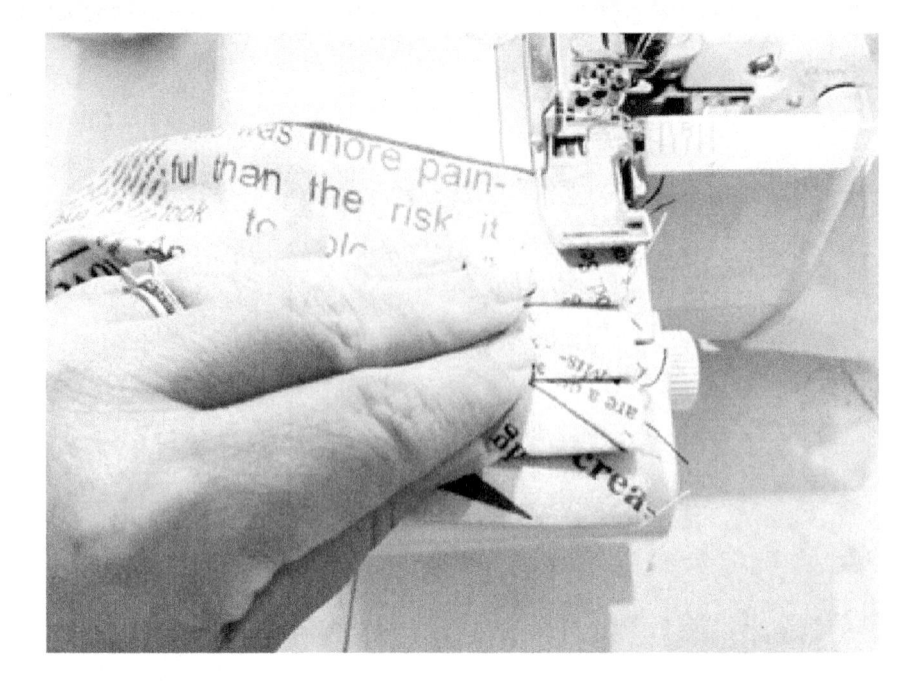

Do the same procedure to the other short side of the mask

Step 10

Trim off the extra threads from your mask. Make sure you tie a knot at the chain of threads before you cut them to secure the seam. Alternatively, you can use a large needle to tuck the chain of threads into the seam.

Step 11

Create a tunnel to secure the strap into your mask. Turn the sides of the mask to the back by about ½ inch and press. Since it is difficult to thread an elastic or knit strap over the pleated tunnel, the ½ inch space will be of great help.

Press the seam or pin it though the pins are not necessary at this time. It will be much faster to stitch without the pins. All you need is to turn the sides of the mask and hold the seam with your fingers.

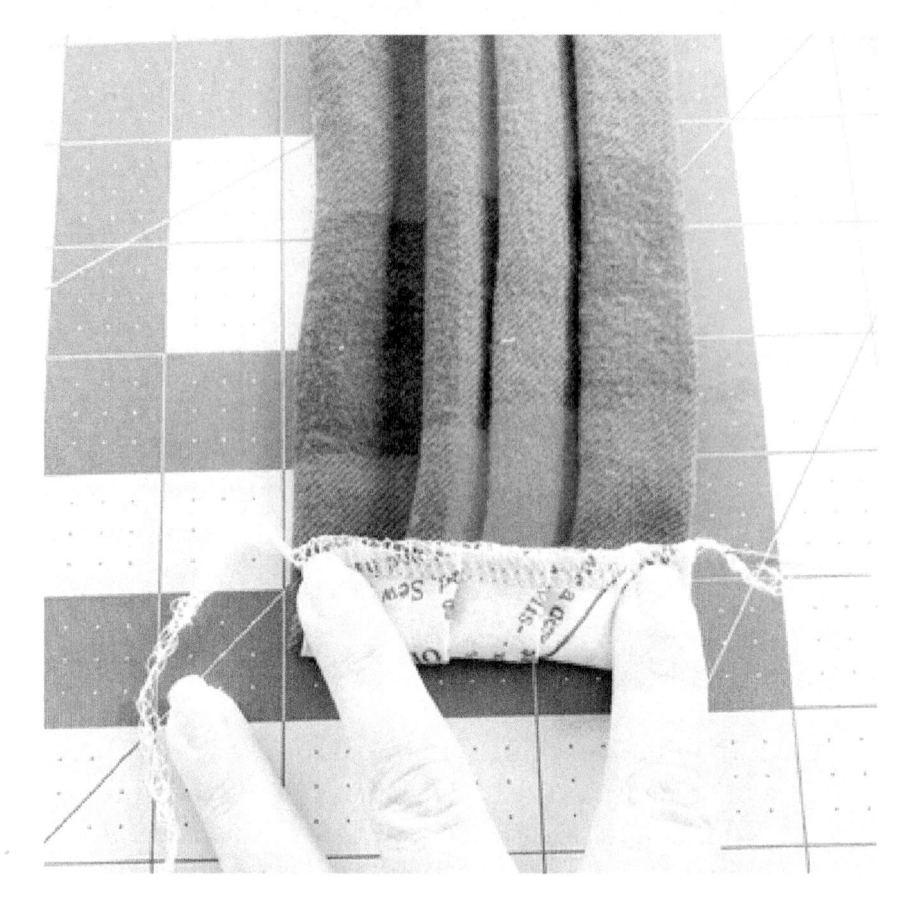

Step 12

Stitch a single seam around the serged threads. Serge from the back of the fabric to make it easy to capture the whole length of the mask on the sides.

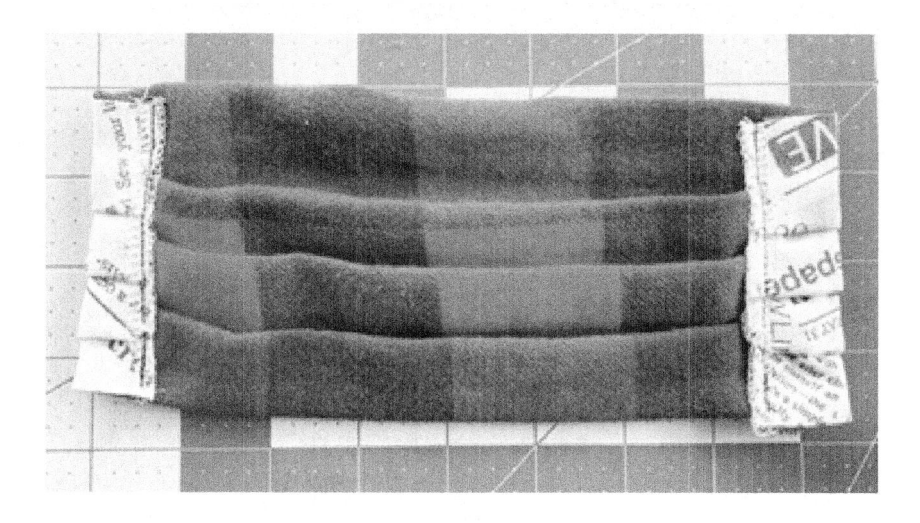

Step 13

Stitch the strap to the fabric. You can use elastic cording, or knit strapping 1 inch wide. If you don't have an elastic or knit fabric, you can cut 1 inch strips from a t-shirt and use them to make the straps for your mask.

Before you fix the straps, place the mask with the front side up and the top side of the mask up.

Step 14

Use the safety pin to securely fix the strap into the mask. Securely pin the end of the strap with the safety pin then use the safety pin to run the strap through the tunnel on the side of the fabric.

Step 15

Insert the safety pin at the tunnel on the bottom right-hand side of the mask. Wiggle the safety pin inside the tunnel until you can pull it at the top of the tunnel. Don't pull the pin through the tunnel.

Insert the pin from the top left side and continue wiggling until you grab it on the other side. This will leave you with a strap connected across the top of the mask and two loose straps hanging at the bottom side of the mask.

Step 16

Remove the safety pin and your mask is ready for use. Once you wear the mask, you can adjust the straps to comfortably fit you. Tie the bottom straps at the back of your head. If the strap is long, you can cut the excess strap.

Alternatively, you can cut the strap at the top side then tie the top piece with the bottom piece on each side to form straps you can wear around your ears. The choice is yours.

It is very easy to make the mask with your serger machine. You only need to learn the basics and you're good to go.

Tips to speed up face mask sewing

1. Start by creating an assembly-line style for your face mask. This involves cutting the fabric into pieces and aligning them so that the pieces can match each other. The assembly line style helps you reduce the number of times you have to stand up from the chair to pick something. If you have several masks to serge, prepare the pieces, and then sew them one after the other. Do not cut the threads until you have sewn all the masks. This saves you a lot of time!

2. You can skip pinning the pieces of fabric together. Instead, fold and use steam to press the pieces. The steam holds the shape in place making it easy to stitch the fabric.

3. Use your serger machine to form the pleats and create a strap tunnel at the same time. In just a single step you can create pleats and tunnel

4. You can serger the top and bottom edges of the mask on the right sides out without using the nose shaper. This eliminates the need for you to turn the mask right side out and press the tube.

5. Get the assistance of making the straps from your family members.

Mask evaluation

The World Health Organization recommends the use of different types of masks depending on where you go, who you are, and the amount of cases of the virus circulating in that area.

You can wear a fabric mask when carrying out your daily chores unless you're interacting with a high-risk group, for example, if you find yourself in a crowded area where there is poor ventilation. You should wear a surgical mask if you're taking care of an ill family member, if you have an underlying medical condition, and if you're above 60 years of age.

Depending on any of the conditions, make sure you wear the right type of mask to protect yourself.

According to CDC guidelines, a good face mask should have at least two layers and be easy to wash without any damage. To know whether you have made the right mask for yourself, use a candlelight test.

The efficiency of the mask is determined by the mask's weave. It should have a tight weave to prevent light from showing through. It should also be thick enough such that you can't blow a candle when wearing the mask

Mask maintenance

You should wash the mask regularly. You can wash them with your regular laundry, using regular laundry detergent. Based on the type of fabric used to make the mask, you can use an appropriate warmest water setting. You should also use the highest heating and leave the mask in the drier to completely dry out.

Chapter Summary

Making your own face mask is a great way to protect yourself and your family. Currently, masks are being used as a comprehensive strategy measure to reduce the transmission of disease and save lives.

When using a mask, ensure it covers your nose, mouth, and your chin in order to get maximum protection from them.

Since you're required to wear a mask daily, making your own mask can help cut costs. You can also make fashionable masks that match your daily outfit.

It is very easy to make your own face mask. In our tutorial, we have discussed two designs you can use to make your own mask. If you have any scrap fabric at home, use it to make custom-made a mask for yourself and your family. You can also make a mask as a gift to your friends. You can make a complete mask within 10 minutes or less based on your design.

Final Words

Serger machines are more preferred than a regular sewing machine because they're much faster. The motor not only runs faster but the machine produces more stitches. Serger machines can create different types of stitches, allowing you to perform several tasks simultaneously.

Apart from creating seams in the fabric, it trims excess fabric and overcast. Due to the various functions, they're preferred for excellent results and ease of use.

When creating stitches, there are different types of stitches you can create with your serger machine. In the above projects, we have used 4-thread stitches on woven and knit fabrics. The 3-thread overlock stitch has been great for creating curved seams and also for the professional finishing of the raw edges of woven fabrics. In most of the projects, we have alternated between the three-thread and four-thread overlock stitch.

For example, our first project was using the blind hem technique to create nearly an invisible seam on the outside of your garment. The stitches are hidden under the folded edges of your fabric.

You can easily join two pieces of raw edges using the blind hemstitch. If you want to attach a pocket to your garment or you simply want to add hemming to your garment, this stitch will give you a neat and clean finish. Blind hem stitches are created using a bling hem foot. Learning how to use this foot will be a great advantage for your serging projects. With the foot, you're able to create super-fast hems that have a professional look.

Another type of stitch you can create for lightweight fabrics is the rolled hemstitch. Serging rolled edges is one of the greatest and fastest hemming techniques you can apply to obtain professional finishings. Rolled hems help you create professional finishing on lightweight and medium weight fabrics. If you're serging a sheer fabric or you want to hem the edges of a scarf or chiffon blouse, then rolled hems will do marvelous work for you.

When using a rolled hem foot, you can use both three-thread stitches. However, some machines will allow you to do rolled hems using a 2-thread overlock stitch although the hem will not be as strong as that done by the 3-thread overlock stitch.

If you're dealing with curved seams like those applied on necklines or armscyes, you can use narrow stitches.

A narrow stitch will result in having a smooth curve since you will have less clipping of the raw edges and notching in order to achieve an efficient turn on your garment.

You're also able to learn how to use the gathering foot to create excellent gathers for your skirts and other garments. This serging tool will make your gathering much easier and you will be able to generate even gathers for your garment. The gathering foot not only helps you to create neat gathers but also helps you to create fabric ruffles.

The gathering foot resembles your regular presser foot but it automatically gathers ruffles as you stitch your fabric, saving you a lot of time and energy. You can use your gathering foot in three ways: to gather ruffle, to shirr your fabric using elastic thread, and to gather ruffle while at the same time you create seams on the non-ruffled fabric. The shirring effect improves the texture of your fabric and makes it look more beautiful.

Depending on the stitch length of your machine, you can create long or small gathers. If the stitch length is short, then you will have small gathers in your garment and vice versa. If you need fuller gathers, you have to set the highest stitch length and increase the differential feed. When adjusting the stitch settings, you can use a piece of scrap fabric to test the stitches. If you have loose threads, adjust them accordingly so that you have a balance of the threads and the stitches. Only when you're satisfied with the stitch setting can you begin your gathering. Otherwise, if you have a gathering fabric at the same time create a seam on non-gathered fabric, you will have a garment with loose stitches that come off when pulled.

Once you have learned how to use your serger machine and serge different types of stitches, you need to learn how to maintain the machine. As we have discussed, you have to clean and oil your machine on a regular basis to boost the life-time of your machine. Proper maintenance ensures your overlock machine remains functional and you don't have any issues with the breaking of needles or threads.

Overlock maintenance involves cleaning, removing lints and pieces of threads, and oiling the movable parts of your serger machine. Not all overlock machines require oiling so you should confirm with your machine manual what type of lubricant or oil to use. Most of the machines come with a soft nylon brush to clean the insides of the machine. You can also use a narrow paint brush to clean around the feed dogs and under the needle plate. Changing needles is also another part of maintaining your machine. You should change them often.

You were also able to learn how to make baby blankets that are more personal between you and your baby. There are different types of materials you can use to make a warm blanket for your baby. Making your own baby blanket gives you the freedom to choose your own design and style. You can also incorporate cartoon themed fabrics to make the blankets.

There are different designs you can choose from and sizes that suit your needs. You can make a blanket with rounded corners or even add embroidery to the top fabric. Always make sure you use the recommended baby clothing fabrics because they're very soft for your baby. You can also make a baby blanket as a gift to your friends.

In Chapter Five, you're able to learn how to make your own pillow covers. Making a pillow cover is effortless and you can personalize them based on your preferences. You don't have to rely on hem tape covers with bulging seams. You can easily make a zippered pillow cover using your machine. Serger machine makes it easy to add zippers so it doesn't have to be scary.

The advantage of making your own pillow covers is that you can select the best fabric that complements your living space. With more practice, you can make pillow covers with different patterns and colors for your living room. Use invisible zippers to make the cover look neat and professional. Home décor fabrics are great for making your pillow covers because of their thicker material that maintains the cover's great shape.

Use a matching thread to stitch the cover and have pillow inserts proportional to the size of your pillow cover so that it can look good on your sofas.

Another DIY sewing project you're able to learn is making a drawstring bag. The drawstring can be great for holding smaller items, using them as a picnic bag, or use the bag to separate different types of clothing when traveling. You can use this bag when going to parties, games, gym or give it as a gift during birthday parties or baby showers.

Making your own drawstring bag is very easy and doesn't need a lot of fabric. You can use scraps of fabric left after making your garment to make the drawstring.

Drawstring bags have wide uses and you can make different sizes that suit different occasions. Different types of fabrics are used to make these types of bags. Make your own stylish designs drawstring bag that you can bring with you at any event. If you're using ribbon pieces as straps to your drawstring bag, then apply fray check at the cut ends of the ribbon to prevent unraveling.

Alternatively, you can make drawstrings with a box bottom. The box bottom makes it easy to place the drawstring on any flat surface. Box bottom requires you to clip part of the fabric to avoid any creases when you stitch the seam around the bottom edges of your drawstring bag. Box bottom drawstring bags look awesome.

We also learned how to make a snack bag that you can bring with you anywhere. If you love going on a picnic, a snack bag will be great for packing different types of snacks. A snack bag can also be referred to as a sandwich bag.

If you pack snacks for your children when going to school then you need one or more snack bags. Making your own snack bag enables you to add a personal touch to them and you will pack fruits and other snacks for your children with a lot of love.

Your children can also choose the design and favorite color for their snack bags. The bags are also eco-friendly and re-usable. You can make different sizes of snack bags to pack different types of snacks.

You can also make snacks using microwave-safe fabrics and that you can dish wash anytime. You can also choose colors that match your outfit.

You have had your serging machine for a while now and having a dust cover will help extend the lifetime of your machine. When you're not using your machine, you should cover it to prevent the accumulation of dust.

Learning to make your own dust cover is very important. Although you can buy a dust cover in the market, you may not get the right size for your machine. Making your own dust cover makes it easy to choose a fabric and color that complements your sewing room. You can make your dust unique and add some pockets that you can store small serger tools or accessories. You also have the freedom to choose the best fabric for your dust cover.

Following the above-discussed steps will help you create your own customized dust cover that suits your serger machine.

In the next chapter, we have talked about how to make a Christmas stocking for your loved ones. Christmas stocking is a large sock crossed with a bag that is used to store gifts from Father Christmas. Children hang Christmas stockings in their room during Christmas Eve because they believe Santa will fill them with gifts if they have behaved well throughout the year.

Instead of buying Christmas stockings for your family, you can make a custom made Christmas stocking. Making the stocking is very easy and cheap and you can make the size as big as you want.

When sewing around the toe curve, cut notch curves so that your stocking looks neat when you turn right side out. You should also avoid clipping the seams around the curve. After making the stocking, you can add a decorative stitch to make the stocking look more attractive. Creating a hanger for your stocking makes it easy to hang it anywhere.

Christmas is here and learning how to make a holiday napkin tree will make your dining table look great. You can create your own modern napkins then transform them into a Christmas tree. If you don't have enough time to make your own napkin, you can use existing napkins and make a Christmas tree with them. These Christmas tree napkins make your dining table look welcoming and your guests will be happy to have them.

When creating your own napkins, you can do it in two ways: creating reversible napkins or creating mitered napkins. Reversible napkins are great for adding color to your dining table and you can use any of the sides while mitered napkins have hemmed edges and are mostly made from linen material.

For you to fold a napkin tree, you need napkins made of natural fibers such as cotton and linen or a blend of cotton and polyester. This will help make it add folds and you don't have to worry about the napkins unfolding themselves when you press them together. The explained steps will guide you in making an excellent Christmas tree napkin. You can also add a bow at the peak and a cinnamon stick at the bottom to make the napkin resemble a real tree. Having several napkins set on your dining table can complement your dining décor.

Lastly, we learned how to create a face mask. Face masks have a variety of uses but currently, we are using face masks to protect ourselves against COVID 19. Since you're required to use masks every day, learning how to make them is very beneficial.

You can make fashionable homemade masks for your family and friends. There are different designs you can use to make the face mask, you can practice several designs and go for the ones you feel comfortable with. Make sure the mask you make has at least two layers for them to give you the protection you deserve. You can also make a face mask with three layers, you only need to make sure the materials used are breathable.

Since most of the face masks sold at the market are for adults, you can make smaller masks for your children. Children below two years are not supposed to wear a face mask.

If you have a scrap fabric at home, use it to make a face mask that matches your outfit. You can make several of them depending on the number of family members. Once you use the mask, you should wash it just like you would wash a regular laundry and dry them.

When cutting the pieces, you can use downloadable online patterns to help you quickly cut the pieces you need for your face masks. There are different patterns you can download, just find the one equivalent to the type and design of mask you want to make and use it to cut the fabric for your new face masks. Sew several of them and donate some to your friends.

With these simple steps, you can create great projects with your server machine. It is also easy and fast compared to a regular sewing machine.

Projects created with a serger machine have a more professional look. Learning the basics of serging will enable you to create more DIY projects. You no longer have to spend money buying various garments. You can create your own customized garments at home.